This book may be kept

SELECTED POEMS OF
HORACE

SELECTED POEMS OF

HORACE

With an Introduction by

GEORGE F. WHICHER

Published for the Classics Club ® by

WALTER J. BLACK, INC. · ROSLYN, N. Y.

On Sabine Hills

On Sabine hills when melt the snows,
　Still level-full his river flows;
Each spring-tide now his valley fills
With cyclamen and daffodils;
And summers wither with the rose.

Swift-waning moons the cycle close:
Birth,—toil,—mirth,—death; life onward goes
Through harvest heat or winter chills
　　On Sabine hills.

Yet One breaks not his long repose,
Nor hither comes when zephyr blows;
In vain the spring's first swallow trills;
Never again that Presence thrills;
One charm no circling season knows
　　On Sabine hills.

GEORGE MEASON WHICHER

Acknowledgments

Permission has been granted by the following authors and publishers to reprint translations to which they hold copyright:

Barclay's Bank, Ltd.: A. E. Housman, *More Poems* (1936)— Odes IV, 7, Dust and Dreams.

G. Bell and Sons, London: H. E. Butler, *The Odes of Horace in English Verse* (1929)—Anonymous, Odes I, 18, The Virtues of the Vine.

Cambridge University Press, Cambridge: Hugh MacNaghten, *The Odes of Horace Done Into English Verse* (1926)—Odes I, 25, To a Faded Beauty; Odes IV, 8, The Gift of the Muse; Odes IV, 15, Thanksgiving for Peace; Odes III, 11, A Tale to Touch the Heart; Odes II, 15, Wealth Encroaches; Odes III, 5, The True Roman Temper.

Henry Harmon Chamberlin: *Horace Talks,* privately printed (1940)—Satires I, 6, Good Birth—And What of It!

Doubleday and Company, Inc.: Franklin P. Adams, *In Other Words* (1912)—Odes I, 8, Getting Lydia's Number; *Toboganning on Parnassus* (1911)—Odes III, 9, The Reconciliation: A Modern Version; Odes III, 15, To Be Quite Frank.

Harcourt, Brace and Company, Inc.: Louis Untermeyer, *Including Horace* (1919)—Odes I, 32, To His Lyre; Epode 7, Civil War; Odes III, 7, "Tears, Idle Tears"; Odes III, 20, "The Female of the Species"; Epode 10, A Pleasant Voyage for Maevius.

Houghton, Mifflin Company: John Osborne Sargent, *Horatian Echoes* (1893)—Odes I, 1, Vocation; Odes IV, 2, No Pindaric Strain; Odes IV, 4, An Eagle of the Claudian Race; Odes IV, 14, Drusus and Tiberius; Odes II, 6, Retirement; Odes I, 4, Returning Spring.

Longmans, Green and Co., Inc.: Alexander Falconer Murison, *Horace Rendered Into English Verse* (1931)—Epode 9, At the Battle; The Secular Hymn; Epode 17, Poet and Witch; Grant

Showerman, *Horace and His Influence* (1922)—Odes III, 30, His Monument.

Alfred A. Knopf: Warren H. Cudworth, *The Odes and Secular Hymn of Horace* (1917)—Odes III, 14, The Return of Augustus; Odes I, 26, In Praise of Lamia; Odes IV, 11, Maecenas' Birthday. James Maclehose and Sons, Glasgow: A. L. Taylor, *The Odes of Horace Translated into English Verse* (1914)—Odes I, 37, The Death of Cleopatra; Odes IV, 6, To Apollo; Odes III, 17, A Feast for a Rainy Day.

Macmillan Company, London: Edward Marsh, *The Odes of Horace* (1943)—Odes III, 19, A Truce to History; Odes I, 7, Come Home to Tibur; Odes I, 29, A Scholar Goes to War; Odes III, 12, The Roman Debutante. Arthur S. Way, *The Epodes of Horace* (1898)—Epode 15, The Traitress; Epode 16, The Happy Isles.

Oxford University Press, London: W. S. Marris, *The Odes of Horace* (1912)—Odes II, 19, Bacchus the Divine; Odes III, 8, The Anniversary; Odes I, 22, Integer Vitae. Austin Dobson, *Poems* —Odes III, 23, Rustic Phidyle; Odes I, 33, Love Mocks Us All; Odes I, 23, To Chloe; Odes III, 10, Impatient; Odes III, 26, We Loved of Yore; Odes I, 38, Persicos Odi; Pocket Version; Odes I, 11, To Leuconoë.

Mrs. Keith Preston: Keith Preston, *Pot Shots from Pegasus* (1929)—Odes I, 38, Chicago Analogue.

G. P. Putnam's Sons: John B. Hague, *The Odes and Epodes of Horace*—Odes IV, 5, Prayer for Augustus.

Charles Scribner's Sons: Eugene and Roswell Martin Field, *Echoes from a Sabine Farm* (1895)—Odes I, 35, Ode to Fortune; Odes III, 13, To the Fountain of Bandusia; Odes I, 5, Speaking from Experience; Epode 6, To a Bully; Odes I, 38, The Preference Declared; Epistles I, 20, To His Book; Odes IV, 10, To Ligurinus; Epode 3, A Counterblast Against Garlic. W. E. Gladstone, *The Odes of Horace* (1894)—Odes I, 14, The Ship of State; Odes IV, 9, Undying Words, Undying Worth.

Introduction

HORATI FLACCI UT MEI ESTO MEMOR

Maecenas to Augustus.

Two thousand years ago a Roman bill-collector in the provincial town of Venusia (about where you would place the ankle in boot-like Italy) was taking extraordinary pains and drawing heavily on his resources to secure a superior education for his son. No school for the heirs of centurions and local bigwigs would do; the boy must go to Rome to study under the best masters the capital afforded. So up the Appian Way journeyed father and son, and in Rome the boy became a pupil of the grammarian Orbilius, who drilled the young patricians of the declining Republic in the art of clear expression and the niceties of Greek. This Orbilius, a celebrated teacher, is said to have practiced his calling with "more reputation than remuneration" and to have composed a small treatise "on the wrongs which schoolmasters suffered at the hands of parents." On both scores he deserves to be kindly remembered.

The country boy from Venusia, like his well-to-do schoolmates, was attended by a suitable retinue of slaves as he went about the city and was accompanied also by a guardian or supervisor of studies. For him, however, this last humble office was not discharged by a trusted servant but by his own father. Under the careful tutelage of the older man the youth was trained to take the utmost advantage of his opportunities. He was encouraged to observe for himself, to reflect upon what he had seen and heard, to distinguish what should be imitated and what avoided in the conduct of his fellows, and so to form for himself a personal standard of values.

Athens, not Rome, was then regarded as the cultural center of Mediterranean civilization, and to Athens accordingly the young man went, after his schooldays at Rome were over, to engage in some further years of study. The son of Cicero, the great orator, and many other young Romans of distinguished family were among his contemporaries there. It was conventional for the students to immerse themselves in the teachings of the Epicurean and Stoic philosophers. One pupil of Orbilius, we may be sure, did not neglect the chance to read with close attention the works of Archilochus, Alcaeus, and other writers who represented the fountainhead of Greek lyric poetry.

What was the reason for this heavy investment in liberal education for a boy who was decidedly of lowly origin? The father who so cheerfully bore the expense was socially a nobody—a freedman, formerly a slave of the municipality. Presumably he could not have failed to be aware that a man of humble birth could only under the most exceptional circumstances attain a high position in the Roman world. We do not know whether his own craving for a cultivated mind led him to seek a vicarious fulfillment through his son, or whether some early signs of promise in the boy revealed a talent that might justify unusual attention. We know only that the magnanimous venture resulted in unqualified success. In later life the freedman's son became an intimate friend of the most prominent men in Rome, among them the pure-souled Virgil, the farseeing and statesmanlike Maecenas, and the all-powerful Augustus Caesar. Through the ages since, moreover, his writings have made him the favorite poet of highly civilized men everywhere, the most frequently quoted and translated of Roman authors, the touchstone of good sense in art as in life. For two thousand years the world has honored the poet Horace.

Quintus Horatius Flaccus, to give him his full name, lived from the year 65 B.C. to the year 8 B.C. He was born a subject of an ancient city-republic at a time when it was plagued by civil wars and crumbling to its end. Before his death he saw Rome regenerated and transformed into the capital of a mighty empire which dominated the known world. In the tumultuous events of his time he played a precarious minor part. It would have been easy for him to fish in troubled waters, but he refrained from doing so. Instead of seeking wealth or power or public acclaim, he found delight in retirement and in the wise regulation of life. Through the exercise of his talents and with no adventitious helps he made himself respected and sought after by the great. No one, even with the best of educations, could have overcome the handicaps that Horace faced at the start of his career unless he had possessed intrinsic qualities of a high order.

There was no trace of servility in Horace's nature. The district of Apulia where he was born and bred was a home of freedom-loving countrymen of Sabellian stock who were not always submissive to the Roman yoke. As recently as 89 B.C. they had taken part in the Marsic rebellion. The town of Venusia itself had been stormed by the Roman legions of Metellus and three thousand of its citizens reduced to captivity. It is a plausible conjecture that Horace's grandfather or father may have lost his status as a free man at this time. In any event a boy brought up in the next succeeding generation among a sturdy people who had tried to assert their freedom and failed could hardly have helped acquiring a strong love of independence. While he ranged freely over the wooded slopes of Mount Voltur and the cultivated plains below, he acquired also a fondness for country life that never left him. He liked room to turn around. All his life Horace had a man's sized portion of self-respect. But though he could be stiff-necked on occasion, he was by nature genial and affectionate. Everything that we know of him makes it clear that he possessed in an eminent degree the faculty of attracting friends and of keeping those he had made.

Venusia, as a station on the Appian Way, was not out of touch with the currents of Roman life. Traders from the Greek cities of southern Italy on their way to Rome and travelers from the north bound for Tarentum, Brundisium, or Athens commonly spent a night there. The stir of traffic effectually prevented the town from becoming a stagnant backwater. It was a favored spot where Greek and Roman cultures overlapped. In going to Athens for his later studies Horace would not have felt that he was visiting an altogether alien land.

The assassination of Julius Caesar took place when Horace was twenty-one. Thenceforth there was little opportunity for quiet study. Like many of the sons of Roman patricians who were his fellow students, Horace was inclined to take the side of Brutus and Cassius in opposition to the Triumvirs. Brutus himself spent some time in Athens while he was engaged in raising an army for the inevitable trial of strength. In the confusion and necessity of the times he would seem to have exercised little care in the selection of his officers. Horace, in spite of his youth, his humble birth, and his inexperience, secured an appointment as military tribune (about the equivalent of a colonelcy). After some two years with the army he took part in the disastrous battle of Philippi (42 B.C.), from which he escaped ingloriously without his shield. When he managed to make his way back to Italy, he found that his father was dead and his estate sequestrated.

At this lowest ebb of his fortunes Horace in all probability was assisted by powerful friends who had a personal regard for him, since he almost at once secured a clerkship in the quaestor's office (or as we might say, in the treasury department), a position which a young Roman of rank need not have scorned. At this time too he began to put in practice his skill in verse-making, wisely selecting for his first efforts the field of satire rather than the more pretentious realms of epic or dramatic poetry. His success was immediate. Within three years we find Virgil and Varius, the rising court poets of the age, bringing Horace to the notice of Maecenas, the powerful adviser of the young Octavius Caesar. The poet's tongue-tied embarrassment when he first stood in the presence of the great man is described in one of his conversation-pieces in verse (Satires I, 6). But once he was accepted as a friend of Maecenas, Horace's fortune was secure.

After he had frequented the household of Maecenas for some years and his worth had been recognized, he received from his considerate patron the gift of a small estate, his well-loved Sabine Farm, in the hilly region of Tibur (near modern Tivoli) about thirty miles east of Rome. Horace's villa, probably a simple farmhouse, was situated on a steep hillside above the rapid stream of the Digentia. Further on the narrow valley opened out, and in all likelihood the larger farming operations carried out by the proprietor and the four tenants who rented holdings from him were confined to these low-lying fields or to an upland plateau some distance behind the dwelling-house. But one can imagine the gray-leaved olive and the grape married to the elm in friendly proximity to the poet's door, while groves of oaks in the background might afford shelter to goats and the rustic Phidyle who watched them. Not far off was the Bandusian spring. The Sabine Farm enabled Horace to resign his clerkship and to enjoy the complete independence that his spirit craved. It also supplied him with a tranquil retreat where he could refresh himself after crowded days in Rome. He asked no more of the kind gods than this. When he was summoned to be a secretary in the household of Augustus, he ventured an all but impossible refusal and managed to decline the honor so tactfully that he still retained the emperor's favor. Maecenas' last message to his royal master included the words: "Cherish Horatius Flaccus as you would myself."

As the years passed the poet's temper grew mellower, or so we may infer from the increasing urbanity manifested in his successive books. The order in which the several gatherings of Horace's poems were made public is known with reasonable certainty. His earliest collection, which appeared about 35 B.C., consisted of ten Satires (informal essays in verse) reviving the native Roman type of *satura* as it had been practiced a generation before by Lucilius. It was followed some five years later by a second group of six Satires less vehement in tone than the first and tending to contain a large element of moral advice. At about the same time the seventeen Epodes formed a third book. These were brief lyrical pieces fashioned after the Greek pattern of Archilochus, many of them diatribes directed against persons whom Horace did not regard with favor. Two addressed to importunate women are excessively coarse.

Horace was evidently blamed for the sharpness of his invectives, and though he defended himself from his detractors, he showed a reasonable regard for the opinions of mankind by modifying his tone. The two books composed during the first decade of his occupation of the Sabine Farm show the poet at the full maturity of his powers. One was the great collection of his Odes (Books I–III) issued about 23 B.C., the masterpiece for which he is best remembered. The other, published about 19 B.C., was the first series of his Epistles which was made up of twenty graceful letters of friendship liberally salted with moral counsels.

As a poet of assured position, a kind of unofficial laureate after Virgil's death, Horace was appointed by Augustus in 17 B.C. to compose the hymn to Apollo and Diana for the Secular Games, a sacred festival which took place every one hundred and eleven years. The first of the two long poetic discourses which form the second book of the Epistles was also written at the command of the emperor, and the fourth book of the Odes, published probably in 13 B.C., is chiefly notable for the many poems celebrating the triumphs of the imperial arms and the peace by conquest which was Rome's gift to the Mediterranean peoples. The extended letter to the Pisos, known also as the Art of Poetry, may have been the last work that Horace wrote.

The poet has described himself in his middle forties as short of stature and plump, with olive complexion, low forehead, and prematurely graying hair. He confessed that he was fond of basking in the sun. His temper was mercurial, soon moved to anger but as quickly appeased. He never married, and the amatory exploits of his youth may be suspected of being largely fabulous. He speaks of his infatuations for sundry women very much as one might mention a change from one brand of tobacco to another. When we encounter him journeying to Brundisium about 37 B.C., we find him already at the age of twenty-eight troubled with sore eyes and something of an invalid. Later in life he was accustomed to spend the winters in the mild climate of Tarentum under doctor's orders. It is far easier to imagine Horace urging his bob-tailed mule to the seclusion of his beloved Sabine hills than hastening in the other direction to keep an appointment with any Lydia or Pyrrha in the gay world of Rome.

As a devoted and loyal friend of his patron, Horace had prayed that he might not be separated from Maecenas by death, and he was not disappointed. He died at the age of fifty-seven, only a few weeks after his benefactor. Both together were buried in Maecenas' gardens on the Esquiline hill. Tradition still points to the supposed tomb of Virgil at Naples, but the site of Horace's grave is unknown. He predicted truly that his poems would outlast enduring brass and princely monuments.

Horace's achievement may be considered first of all in relation to his historical setting. He was one of the foremost poets of the Augustan Age, a member of the brilliant coterie who gathered about Maecenas and enjoyed the favor of his imperial master. Each of these writers took as his particular concern one of the principal forms of literary art: Varius was to produce epic poetry, Pollio tragedy, Fundanius comedy, Virgil pastoral and rural poetry, Octavius history, and Horace satire. In time several of the poets modified their original roles, Virgil to surpass Varius in the domain of the epic, Pollio to write the history of the Roman civil wars, and Horace to become a lyric poet. They were singularly free from personal jealousies, perhaps in part because they were bound together and inspired by a common loyalty to their vision of empire. They saw Rome in the past as a city of destiny, and they projected far into the future its mission as the power that was to bring sanity and peace to a distracted world. Augustus they glorified as the incarnation of the imperial policy. They were ambitious to implement and ornament his reign by fostering the beliefs that were needed in the creation of a new form of society.

Virgil's magnificent embodiment of the myth of Roman grandeur in the epic of Trojan Aeneas is rightly regarded as the supreme poetic masterpiece of the Augustan period. It holds in pure heroic form the ideal values envisioned in the conception of the empire. It remains an imperishable symbol of human striving to achieve a destiny so great that all personal considerations seem petty in comparison. Yet for a picture of the kind of life that Romans were living while Augustus was founding the empire, for sketches of manners and customs, for impressions of many sorts of men and women, for gaieties and gravities combined, not without the perception of deeper currents of feeling and the poignance of the human lot, we must turn to Horace. He is the poet who meets us on the level of everyday concerns. He is the one who convinces us that the people of two thousand years ago were once as vitally alive as we.

In his first Satires Horace wrote of the varied world of Rome somewhat tentatively, without any apparent guiding aim. Sometimes he attacked its degeneracy and corruption, sometimes he recorded a realistic personal impression as of his journey to Brundisium, sometimes he created an episode of social comedy as in his encounter with the bore, or again he would produce a trifle for sheer entertainment like his account of Priapus and the witches. At this period of his career he had not acquired polarity. Had he possessed a reforming temper, however, the satiric vein might have led him on to fiercer and fiercer denunciations. But Horace was not by nature a Juvenal or a Jeremiah.

He was not indifferent to the program for the regeneration of the Roman body politic which Augustus inaugurated as soon as his victories over Cleopatra and Sextus Pompeius left him free to turn to domestic matters. Horace's response, characteristically, was intensely moral and practical. In support of the imperial reforms he wrote a series of Odes on national questions, denouncing the growing luxury of Roman life and calling on his countrymen to revive the virtues of their ancestors. These Odes, particularly the group of six that stand together at the beginning of Book III, gave powerful expression to capacities in Horace's nature which his adaptations of Greek lyrics could never have released. His assertion of ultimate devotion to the state, the supreme Roman virtue, was needed to give a note of firmness and dignity to his poetry. Without such patriotic fervor Horace's Odes would not command the full respect of a masculine audience.

Yet deeply as Horace was moved by patriotic, moral, and religious themes, we do not feel that the essence of his poetic gift is contained in these semi-official endorsements of imperial policy. The aspect of his work which has most appealed to succeeding ages is that which transcends the conditions of his time. Horace is a great poet because men feel that in him the potential qualities of human nature found unusual fulfillment, both in terms of art and in terms of a critical evaluation of life.

After he had tried with some success to imitate in Latin epodes the "sharp iambics" of Archilochus, Horace conceived the design of reproducing in his own tongue the exquisite beauty of Greek lyric poetry, passing over with a sure instinct for the best the productions of the recent Alexandrian school and returning to the antique perfection of Alcaeus and Sappho. Poetry for him, therefore, was not as for Catullus or Robert Burns a channel for the outpouring of immediate personal longings and dislikes. It was rather what poetry must have been for Dryden pre-eminently among English writers—a problem in craftsmanship. The poet's whole being could be concentrated on finding appropriate and tasteful expression. His subjects, though possibly confirmed in his own experience, were typically not personal to him, but were rather the property of poets in all ages. Without seeking for peculiar novelties, therefore, Horace became a supreme master of the felicitous and apt phrase. The resulting Odes, though easily comprehensible to all men, are never commonplace. Their sure and exquisite artistry brings them so close to perfection that they have remained the admiration of connoisseurs from Horace's day to this.

In a more personal and private vein Horace composed his Epistles, protesting that they were meant only for the eyes of a few favored friends, not for the world at large. The informal style suited perfectly his genius for a frank and ingratiating address, whether he wrote to ask news of a friend, to invite him to supper, or to proclaim himself jocularly "a porker from the sty of Epicurus." Horace's unassuming modesty is especially apparent in these poems, though more or less diffused through all his writing. He was a lovable person.

Men have valued his poetry in last analysis because they have recognized in him a man who has achieved a sound sense of values. His judgment inspires confidence. He believed in what he had tested and found good. He was skeptical of what the crowd desired. He had strength of mind, like Thoreau, to live alone, to withdraw from the pursuit of vulgar satisfactions and to find contentment in moderation. He practiced equally a wise indulgence and a wise restraint, accepted without repining his limitations, and was tolerant of life's inevitable shortcomings. In a word, Horace impresses us as a man who thoroughly understood the art of living. Through his power to shape into artistic form thoughts and feelings not alien to the generality of men he attained an intensity of being which we recognize at once as the mark of a genuine poet. Like other men of genius he leaves us a hope that the possibilities inherent in humanity may be ever more fully realized. Our lives are the larger for his having lived.

Horace's works were known throughout the Middle Ages, but unlike Virgil's *Aeneid* his poems did not lend themselves through allegory to Christian interpretation. After Virgil, Dante's guide and master, Ovid was the favorite classical poet of medieval readers. Horace remained one of the "good Pagans," whose ethical teachings, though not illuminated by divine inspiration, might be accepted with due caution. His unethical lyrics were sometimes deprecated but no doubt enjoyed. Complete and sympathetic understanding of Horace dates from the Renaissance.

At about the same time translations and imitations of his work in English began to appear. Since the humanists of the sixteenth century were well prepared to appreciate the doctrine of the Golden Mean, it was no accident that the Ode (II, 10) in which Horace most directly states the central canon of his philosophy should have been twice translated, once by Surrey and once by Sidney. From the time of Queen Elizabeth, herself an unsuccessful translator of the Art of Poetry, new translations of particular poems, of the Odes as a whole, and less frequently of the Satires, Epodes, and Epistles, have been produced in almost every decade, nor is there any indication at present of a slackening of effort. The rendering of Horace into English has long been a standard avocation of both professional poets and amateurs of letters. If the eighteenth century specialized most diligently in Horatian paraphrase and adaptation, the nineteenth and twentieth centuries have been equally industrious in the attempt to capture the exact shadings of his meaning in every conceivable style of translation.

An anthology of Horace's poems in English versions, therefore, may fairly make a virtue of variety. It should represent a large number of translators from different periods and should avoid giving undue weight to any single fashion or school. Rather it should attempt to display the full richness of the Horatian legacy to English verse. To accomplish this most readily more than one rendering of certain favorite poems should be chosen, so that a seventeenth or eighteenth century version may be directly compared with a modern one, a literal translation with a paraphrase, a redaction in formal language with a skit in the vernacular. In the present volume the reader may find both profit and entertainment in comparing Thomas Campion and John Quincy Adams on *Integer vitae* (Odes I, 22) or Robert Herrick and Franklin P. Adams on *Donec gratus eram* (Odes III, 9) or Dr. Johnson and A. E. Housman on *Diffugere nives* (Odes IV, 7). To give an example in brief of the possible derivatives from a single original the editor has included seven versions of the tiny *Persicos odi* (Odes I, 38) by authors ranging from William Cowper to the late Chicago columnist Keith Preston.

In making a choice of translations from the embarrassing number available the editor has given priority to the occasional pieces produced by well-known poets, and he has intentionally played down the work of professional translators. This book accordingly has been built around a core of poems written by poets famous in their own right. The list includes Ben Jonson, Milton, Cowley, and Dryden from the seventeenth century, Congreve, Swift, Pope, Samuel Johnson, and Cowper from the eighteenth, and Hartley Coleridge, Leigh Hunt, C. S. Calverley, Matthew Arnold, Austin Dobson, and A. E. Housman from the period since 1800. Besides the poets, novelists are represented by Thackeray and Bulwer-Lytton, statesmen by John Quincy Adams and William E. Gladstone, and clergymen and schoolteachers by a throng too numerous to particularize. Here will be found the first American translator, John Parke, and his contemporary Susanna Rowson, author of the ever popular romance of *Charlotte Temple* and the only woman contributor. A relatively large number of pieces have been taken from the translators of selected Odes, among whom may be mentioned Francis S. Mahoney ("Father Prout"), Branwell Brontë, the ill-fated brother of the noted sisters, Eugene Field and his brother Roswell, and Mr. Louis Untermeyer. Chinks and crevices in the structure thus composed were finally filled by specimens from the more spirited translators of the Odes or the complete works of Horace from Philip Francis to Sir Edward Marsh.

The editor has drawn freely upon translations published by his father and himself more than a quarter of a century ago, and has written especially for this volume new versions of Odes I, 11 and 38, and of Satires I, 8.

For nearly two thousand years Horace's poems have always been presented in the order which the poet himself established. The arrangement was carefully contrived, though it avoided the appearance of being systematic. He saw to it that the opening poem in his collected Satires, Epodes, Odes, and Epistles, respectively, should be addressed to Maecenas in order that his patron might be duly honored. Certain poems to Augustus Caesar were also given strategic positions. The third book of the Odes and the first book of the Epistles closed with poems that reviewed the writer's achievements. But aside from special placing of certain poems, the general effect that Horace sought to secure was one of constant variety. Except for the six national Odes at the beginning of Book III, he seldom allowed two poems on the same theme to appear in close conjunction. In this way he kept the reader's attention fresh, set off contrasting poems, and made the most of the relatively small number of poetic themes to which he recurred over and over again.

By regrouping the poems under topical headings, as has been done in the present volume, it is possible to bring out certain values that are less apparent when the poems are mingled in artfully artless confusion. Relationships between two or more pieces may be emphasized, and comparisons of poems of a similar kind may readily be made. All the Odes and Epodes but five have here been assembled under eight general headings, and with them have been included four of the shorter Epistles and one Satire. A ninth section contains a few further specimens of Horace's conversation-pieces, both Satires and Epistles together. Tenth and last comes the Art of Poetry by itself as the most famous example of Horace's work as a literary critic. The new arrangement is not offered as an improvement on the poet's own, but it may have at least the value of novelty. By placing the poems in a fresh context it is hoped that unsuspected facets of Horace's genius may be brought to light and that English readers may experience anew the pleasure which students of Latin have taken for many centuries in verse at once familiar and yet never stale.

GEORGE F. WHICHER

Contents

WITCHES, HAGS, AND OTHER
  ABHORRENCES   135

THE GOLDEN MEAN   155
Praise of Meane and Constant

SELECTED POEMS OF
HORACE

The Poet

Like many other poets ancient and modern, Horace regarded the writing of poetry as a sacred mystery, to be practiced only by those who are supremely consecrated to the art. Poetry, itself an immortal thing, can confer lasting remembrance on whatever it touches. Were it not for poets the greatest heroes would die unsung and hence unhonored. This high appreciation of the poet's calling, though genuinely felt by Horace, was a conventional theme, probably borrowed from the Greek lyrists who were his models.

More particularly his own were the poems in which he defined the exact nature of his accomplishment and indicated the limitations of his powers. In To His Lyre (Odes I, 32) and His Monument (Odes III, 30) he declared that his special achievement consisted in creating in Latin a body of lyric poetry equivalent to that of such admired Greek masters as Alcaeus, Sappho, Anacreon, and Archilochus. He was speaking mainly of the technical feat of writing Latin poetry in the precise and elaborate stanza forms imported from Greece. In that respect Horace's skill was indeed extraordinary. No Latin poet before him had attempted what seemed an impossible piece of literary dexterity, and none since his time has been able to equal the perfection of his work or to master anything like the number of intricate strophes, about twenty in all, that Horace employed. He had good reason to feel proud of what he had done.

But along with a keen sense of his power went a perception of what lay outside the range of his fragile gift. He was conscious that he could not be an epic singer like his friends Virgil and Varius, and that the large themes which called for treatment in the grand style would never do for him. Consequently he was often forced to explain that he was not just a poet of all work, but a specialist in a delicate kind of verse which could be applied only to light and graceful topics. It was not for him to chronicle the

3

glories of Augustus' reign or to celebrate the triumph of Agrippa at the battle of Actium. He could not even claim to be the Pindar of his age.

Toward the end of his career, nevertheless, Horace seems to have yielded reluctantly to pressure and to have composed several odes in honor of Augustus and in praise of the military successes of the emperor's young kinsmen. These dutiful tributes to the head of the Roman state were less characteristic of Horace than the odes picturing the battles of laughing girls and their lovers. The best of his poetry, though devoted to the exquisite elaboration of trifles, was not in itself trivial. The overcoming of difficulties with seemingly effortless grace gave it the dignity of a high art.

To His Book

Epistles I, 20

You vain, self-conscious little book,
   Companion of my happy days,
How eagerly you seem to look
For wider fields to spread your lays;
   My desk and locks cannot contain you,
   Nor blush of modesty restrain you.

Well, then, begone, fool that thou art!
But do not come to me and cry,
   When critics strike you to the heart:
"Oh, wretched little book am I!"
   You know I tried to educate you
   To shun the fate that must await you.

In youth you may encounter friends
(Pray this prediction be not wrong),
   But wait until old age descends
And thumbs have smeared your gentlest song;
   Then will the moths connive to eat you
   And rural libraries secrete you.

However, should a friend some word
Of my obscure career request,
   Tell him how deeply I was stirred
To spread my wings beyond the nest;
   Take from my years, which are before you,
   To boom my merits, I implore you.

Tell him that I am short and fat,
Quick in my temper, soon appeased,
With locks of gray,—but what of that?
Loving the sun, with nature pleased.
I'm more than four and forty, hark you,—
But ready for a night off, mark you!

Roswell Martin Field

To His Lyre

Odes I, 32

Now we are called upon. O lyre,
If ever we in secret here
Have sung one strain that men admire
And may outlive the passing year,
I pray thee tune the throbbing wire
From which my dearest songs have flowed,
And let me build for my desire
A Latin ode.

A Lesbian poet showed us first
Thy passion and thy fluent power;
And in the battle's lust and thirst,
Or quiet of the calmer hour,
He swept the silent strings; he versed
The lovely Venus in her pride;
Or showed us Cupid being nursed
Close at her side.

He chanted Bacchus wondrously;
And, when the Muses' praise was sung,
Extolled the black-eyed Lycus, he
Who was so delicate and young . . .

O thou who art and e'er wilt be
The charm and the delight of all,
Come and be gracious unto me—
Answer the call.

Louis Untermeyer

Melpomene

Odes IV, 3

The man thou hast inspired, Melpomene,
And viewed at hour of birth with serene eyes,
Exalted by thy sovereign power shall be.

No Isthmian games shall hail his victory,
No fleeting chariot bear him to the prize,—
The man thou hast inspired, Melpomene.

No conqueror of haughty monarchs he;
Not he, with brows enwreathed in victors' guise,
Exalted by thy sovereign power shall be.

Where woods are dense and rills fall plenteously,
The soul of song within him glorifies
The man thou hast inspired, Melpomene.

I naught can envy; Rome has honored me.
My lays, by her deemed worthy of the skies,
Exalted by thy sovereign power shall be.

I sing to please thee, Muse, and only thee
In whom the master-gift of music lies.
Exalted by thy sovereign power shall be
The man thou hast inspired, Melpomene.

George F. Whicher

The Poet's Prayer to Apollo
Odes I, 31

When, kneeling at Apollo's shrine
   The bard from silver goblet pours
Libations due of votive wine,
   What seeks he, what implores?

Not harvests from Sardinia's shore;
   Not grateful herds that crop the lea
In hot Calabria; not a store
   Of gold, and ivory;

Not those fair lands where slow and deep
   Thro' meadows rich and pastures gay
Thy silent waters, Liris, creep
   Eating the marge away.

Let him, to whom the Gods award
   Calenian vineyards, prune the vine;
The merchant sell his balms and nard,
   And drain the precious wine

From cups of gold; to Fortune dear
   Because his laden argosy
Crosses, unshattered, thrice a-year
   The storm-vexed Midland sea.

Ripe berries from the olive bough,
   Mallows and endives, be my fare.
Son of Latona! Hear my vow;
   Apollo, grant my prayer,

Health to enjoy the blessings sent
   From heaven; a mind unclouded, strong;
A cheerful heart; a wise content;
   An honoured age; and song.

Sir Stephen Edward De Vere

Vocation

Odes I, 1

Alike my guardian and my grace,
Maecenas, born of Tuscan Kings,
Men live to whom the Olympian race
With clouds of dust its rapture brings;
And when the glowing axles graze
But clear the goal, and win the prize,
The ennobling palm will even raise
Earth's greatest Masters to the skies;
Him who by Rome's capricious choice
Her triple powers and honors wields,
And him whose granaries rejoice
In all the wealth of Libya's fields.
The man who lives contented now
To hoe and delve ancestral acres
No gold will tempt on Cyprian prow
To face Myrtoan storms and breakers.
The merchant, fearing winds and waves,
Praises farm-life and quits the sea,
But soon again its shipwrecks braves,
Untaught to bear with poverty.
This man disdains not to recline
Beneath an arbute half the day,
And quaff his cups of Massic wine,
And doze where sacred fountains play.
Live many men for whom the camp
And trumpet-blast that calls to arms,
The horn's sharp shriek, and war's stern tramp,
Hated by mothers, have their charms.
Unmindful of his tender spouse,
The huntsman fronts the frosty air,
If faithful hounds the deer arouse,
Or wild boar break the well-wrought snare.

Thee, ivies, crown of learned men,
  Mix with celestial gods; with me,
Apart from crowds, in grove and glen
  Satyrs and Nymphs find company—
If sweet Euterpe plays her flute,
  Nor Polyhymnia denies
Her echoes of the Lesbian lute:
  But I shall touch the starry skies
If thou vouchsafe to write my name
  Among the bards of lyric fame.

John Osborne Sargent

To Maecenas

Odes II, 12

No; ask no more so soft a lyre
  As mine to strain its simple wire,
And tell of wild Numantian wars,
Nor Hannibal and all our scars,
Nor yet of that Sicilian tide
With Carthaginian blood bedyed,
Nor of the fierce Pirithoan stir
That crushed the jovial ravisher,
Nor giant sieges of the sky,
Herculean strife, that shook on high
Old Saturn's glorious dynasty.

You, dear Maecenas, shall rehearse
In prose much better than my verse,
The battles that our Caesar gains,
And threatening kings led up in chains:—
Me the fond Muse engrosses still
With my Licymnia's warbling skill,

And those two eyes of cordial fire,
That speak the faith which they inspire.
How lightsome in the dance is she,
How sparkling sweet her raillery,
And what a shape her arm of snow,
When upon days of sacred show
Entwined the glancing maidens go!

Would you, if you adored like me,
For all that Monarchs hold in fee,
Exchange, or even think to share,
One lock of such a charmer's hair,
When back she throws that sweep of bliss
Her neck, to meet a headlong kiss,
Or cruel for relenting's sake,
Denies what you should rather take,—
Turning at last, with smile and start,
And kissing you with all her heart?

Leigh Hunt

To a Roman Historian

Odes II, 1

Pollio! your page records the fate
Of Rome, her crimes, her wars, her feuds,
Their causes and vicissitudes,
Since brave Metellus ruled its state,
The sport of Fortune, the array
Of leaders banded to betray,
And Roman armour crimsoned o'er
With yet unexpiated gore.
A high but perilous task! you tread
O'er fires with treacherous ashes spread.

Forsake the tragic muse severe
Awhile. When your historic pen
Has traced in characters austere
The fates of nations and of men,
Your Attic buskin wear again
Bold pleader of the sufferers' cause;
Champion of Roman arms and laws.
Pollio, the Senate's counsellor,
Crowned hero of Dalmatia's war!

Hark! As I read I seem to hear
The clarion bray; the trumpet's breath
With quivering thunder smites mine ear;
Methinks I see the war-horse quail
Before yon wall of flashing mail,
And warriors, wan with sudden fear,
    Trembling at coming death;
And chiefs careering o'er the plain
With no ignoble battle-stain,
And all that's best on earth subdued
Save Cato's iron fortitude.

Juno and gods who loved the Afric shores,
Yielding reluctant, powerless then to save,
Have laid as victims at Jugurtha's grave
The offspring of his Roman conquerors.
What soil by Daunian carnage fed
Teems not with Latin tombs? What flood
Rolls not unhallowed waters, red
    With fratricidal blood?
The Medes, the Parthians in their desert home
Exulting hear the crash of falling Rome.

Cease, cease, presumptuous shell!
The Cean's lofty dirge beseems thee not.
Once more with me a lighter descant swell
To love and laughter in Dione's grot.

Sir Stephen Edward De Vere

A Truce to History

Odes III, 19

No history, please! Work out some other time
      The pedigree of Aeacus,
Settle the dates of Inachus
And Codrus, in his death sublime.
Even your outline of the Trojan War,
Just now, would be a bore.
Far sooner would we have you say
What price a cask of Chian is today,
Or where, and what o'clock, we dine,
Who warms the water for the wine,
And shields us from this Arctic winter's nip.

Now, boy, the toasts! Murena's augurship!
New Moon! and Midnight! shall the bumpers be
Nine ladlefuls, or three?
Our frenzied bard, the Muses' votary,
Will plump, of course, for nine;
While they who, like the Graces, hate a riot,
Choose three, to keep the table quiet.
   Now we'll go berserk—let the binge begin!
Pipe up, thou Berecynthian flute!
Down from your pegs, ye lyre and lute!
I hate a stingy host like sin.
More roses! wake the neighbours with the din—
Crusty old Lycus and his Pretty Poll,
Who has no use for him at all.
Here Love be lord! flushed Rhoda find her heaven
In Bassus, shining like the star of even
With his bright curly hair; while I
Burning for Chloe, lingeringly die.

Edward Marsh

No Pindaric Strain

Odes IV, 2

He who would walk in Pindar's ways
    Strives for a Daedalean fame;
And on his wings of wax essays
    To give some glassy sea a name.

Like mountain stream that swollen by showers
    From bank and barrier bursts away,
Sublime and deep,—so Pindar pours
    The torrent of his fervid lay.

To him, audacious bard, assign
    Apollo's laurel,—whether he
Dashes in dithyrambic line,
    Rolling new words in numbers free;

Or sings of gods and monarchs who
    The blood of gods as heroes claim,
Who in just rage the Centaurs slew
    And quenched the fell Chimaera's flame;

Or them the Elean palm uplifts
    To feel like gods—the men who vie
In ring or race, and win the gifts
    A hundred statues would not buy;

Or to the stars exalts some youth,
    Snatched from a weeping bride away,
Whose strength and sense and golden truth
    Shall live forever in his lay.

The Theban swan affects the sky,
    And, wafted on the swelling breeze,
Soars through the clouds—but, Antony,
    Like one of Mount Matina's bees

That roams in patient quest of flowers
    Tibur's moist banks and groves along,
So I consume laborious hours
    In fashioning my little song.

But you shall strike with larger quill
    The lyre that sounds with Caesar's praise,
When he ascends the sacred hill,
    Sygambria's victor, crowned with bays:

No better, greater gift, have Fate
    And the good Gods bestowed on earth
Nor will, though they should re-create
    The times that saw its golden birth.

And you shall sing, in lofty strain,
    Of festive days and public sports
For brave Augustus come again—
    Of crowded streets and empty Courts.

With you I then will lift my voice—
    Should words worth hearing come from me;
In Caesar's welcome all rejoice;
    O radiant Sun! All praise to thee!

And as we follow in your train,
    Io Triumphe! we will sing;
Again we'll sing it and again,
    And to kind Gods our incense bring.

Ten bullocks and as many cows
    For you must on the altar bleed;
A little calf will pay my vows,
    That frisks new-weaned upon the mead;

The crescent that adorns his head
    Like the moon's third-day fires is bright;
His color is a tawny red,
    But. where he's marked the spots are white.

John Osborne Sargent

To a Roman Admiral

Odes I, 6

On Homer's wing let Varius sing
    Agrippa, good and brave;
With what his warriors, conquering,
    Have done by land or wave:
But nor to strains like these aspire
Our warblings, nor Pelides' ire
    Can we sublimely tell,
Nor how across old ocean's roar
His course the wise Ulysses bore,
Nor how, defiled with kindred gore,
    The house of Pelops fell.

Nor may our Muse, unwarlike, mar
    With coldly creeping line
The praise of Caesar famed so far,
    Or, great Agrippa, thine!
And who *can* sing the God of war
With bright arms blazing from afar;
    Or Merion famed in fight,
With blackened front and bloody blade;
Or Diomede, by Pallas' aid
    Equal to Gods in might?

No, feasts and frolics be our theme,
    And brimming bowls of wine,
And pleasure's laugh, and beauty's beam,
    And dance and song divine:
We'll sing of virgins' wanton wiles,
Who fight with rage disclosed in smiles,
    And *tempt* the foe to try;
Ourself, as wont, of careless frame,
Whether we feel the general flame,
    Or coldly smile it by.

Patrick Branwell Brontë

"They Had No Poet"
Odes IV, 9

Lest you should think that verse shall die,
 Which sounds the silver Thames along,
Taught on the wings of truth to fly
 Above the reach of vulgar song;

Though daring Milton sits sublime,
 In Spenser native Muses play;
Nor yet shall Waller yield to time,
 Nor pensive Cowley's moral lay.

Sages and chiefs long since had birth
 Ere Caesar was, or Newton named;
These raised new empires o'er the earth,
 And those, new heavens and systems framed.

Vain was the chief's, the sage's pride!
 They had no poet, and they died.
In vain they schemed, in vain they bled!
 They had no poet, and are dead.

Alexander Pope

Undying Words, Undying Worth
Odes IV, 9

Think not these words are doomed to die
 Which, wedded to the tuneful string,
With newborn arts of minstrelsy
 From sounding Aufidus I sing.

If Homer on the throne be set,
    Stesichorus is stately still,
Alcaeus brave; and Pindar yet,
    And Cean song their places fill.

The sportive tales Anacreon told
    Years have not blurred. Love cannot die,
And warms to-day, and warmed of old
    Th' Aeolian maiden's poesy.

Were there like Spartan Helen none
    That loved the trim adulterer's hair,
The gold upon his vestments spun,
    His train, his port, of royal air?

Was Teucer first to learn the use
    Of Cretan shafts? Was Troy subdued
At once? Fought huge Idomeneus,
    Or Sthenelos, in solitude?

War is the Muse's theme. Not first
    Deiphobus, or Hector's rage,
For their pure spouses dared the worst,
    Or did for children battle wage.

Ere Agamemnon saw the light
    There lived brave men: but tearless all,
Enfolded in eternal night,
    For lack of sacred minstrels, fall.

Test hidden baseness, buried worth;
    'Tis little odds. So, Lollius, I
Will set thy deeds and virtues forth;
    Too many and too great to die,

And moulder, dark Oblivion's prey.
    Thou hast a soul for high affairs,
Art formed to hold unchanged thy way,
    When Fortune smiles, or Fortune scares.

O scourge of greed and trick, O freed
From Money's all-absorbing sway,
Who, whensoe'er the state had need,
No consul of the year or day,

Took'st not the useful for the good,
Flung'st back the guilty gift with scorn,
Through adverse hosts along thy way
In Virtue's arms triumphant borne.

Not him wilt thou for happy bless,
Whose goods are large. Far happier he,
Who shall for wisdom's use possess
The bounties that the gods decree.

And pinching poverty can bear,
And baseness more than death can dread.
For love of friends, or country's care,
That man will gladly give his head.

W. E. Gladstone

The Gift of the Muse

Odes IV, 8

I should be sending, Censorinus, gifts,
Bronzes and bowls, to please and suit my friends,
Or tripods, prizes of the gallant Greeks,
And you should have the very best of all,
That is, if I were rich in works of art
Such as Parrhasius or Scopas wrought,
This skilled in stone, that other in soft hues,
To fashion now a man and now a god.
But no such treasure I possess, and you
Have wealth but not the wish for such conceits.

Song is your heart's desire, 'tis mine to give
Song, and to tell the value of the gift.
Not marbles graved with fame for all to read,
Which give to good and gallant chiefs a new
Life after death, not Hannibal's swift flight
And all his threats flung backward in his teeth,
Nor yet the flames of perjured Carthage show
The praise of him who filched from Africa
A surname or illumine valiant deeds
More than the Muses of Calabria:
Nor if the page were mute, would praise be yours
For all your merit. Who would know the boy
Of Ilia and Mars if Silence grudged
Fame to the high deserts of Romulus?
What from the waves of Styx snatched Aeacus?
Valour, and love of men, and sovran song
Enshrine him in those islands richly blest.
The Muse forbids th' heroic soul to die,
The Muse awards heav'n's bliss. Through her, to Jove's
Most blessèd feast came tireless Hercules,
Through her the bright stars, sons of Tyndarus,
Snatch from engulfing waves the shattered barks,
And Liber, with the vine's green wreath around
His brow, to happy issue speeds the prayer.

Hugh MacNaghten

The Poet's Departure

Odes II, 20

No common flight, no weakly wing
    Me, bird and bard at once, shall bear
Through the clear realms of liquid air.
This earth, too great for envy's sting,

And towns, I quit. Maecenas dear,
　Deem not, though humbly born, that I
　Like ordinary folk will die,
And see the Stygian waters drear.
Rough skin already clothes my thighs,
　And all above light feathery down
　From shoulder e'en to finger grown
Makes me a snow-white swan in guise.
Swifter than Icarus my flight
　Shall reach the moaning Bosphorus' shore,
　And Afric's quicksands, and explore
The frozen plains of endless night.
Spain with her lore my song shall own,
　And Colchis, and the tribes that fear,
　But seem to flout, the Marsians' spear,
And all who quaff the stream of Rhone.
Then bid no mournful funeral wail
　My empty obsequies attend:
　Thy grief restrain; nor to thy friend
Pay honors that can nought avail.

Thomas Charles Baring

His Monument

Odes III, 30

Not lasting bronze nor pyramid upreared
　By princes shall outlive my powerful rhyme.
The monument I build, to men endeared,
Not biting rain, nor raging wind, nor time,
Endlessly flowing through the countless years,
Shall e'er destroy. I shall not wholly die;
The grave shall have of me but what appears;
For me fresh praise shall ever multiply.

As long as priest and silent Vestal wind
The Capitolian steep, tongues shall tell o'er
How humble Horace rose above his kind
Where Aufidus' rushing waters roar
In the parched land where rustic Daunus reigned,
And first taught Grecian numbers how to run
In Latin measure. Muse! the honor gained
Is thine, for I am thine till time is done.
Gracious Melpomene, O hear me now,
And with the Delphic bay gird round my brow.

Grant Showerman

The Roman

Horace could hardly have been the friend of Maecenas and of the Emperor Augustus without taking an interest in the violent changes that were shaking the Roman world. First and last he wrote a considerable number of poems on public affairs. When these are arranged in a possible chronological order, they throw a revealing light on the development of the poet's political opinions.

The earliest in date is perhaps the curious piece called The Happy Isles (Epode 16), which announces the impending ruin of the Roman state and summons the cultivated few to leave the unthinking many to destruction. Rather than share their fate, let the exiles set sail for the fabled Hesperides and there establish once more the customs of the Age of Gold. Written shortly after the defeat of Brutus at Philippi, this poem seems to represent the wishful thinking of a baffled republican idealist.

About the time of Horace's introduction to Maecenas may be placed two poems, one (Epode 7) protesting against the senseless renewal of civil disturbances, and the other (Odes I, 14), indicating the poet's growing concern for the safety of the ship of state.

Some eight years later we encounter the poet, now devoted to the service of Maecenas, offering to accompany his patron to the wars, and in the two following poems celebrating the great victory of the young Octavius Caesar over Antony and Cleopatra at the battle of Actium, 30 B.C. Horace, always in theory something of a noble Roman, disliked Egyptian luxury as much as Persian and rejoiced in the utter defeat of the enervating East.

When Octavius assumed the title of Augustus and made himself the sole master of the state, Horace became convinced that the salvation of Rome lay in the emperor's hands. He readily cooperated with the emperor's efforts, about 28 B.C., to revive the traditional worship of the gods and to encourage the heroic virtues of an earlier time. Possibly Horace's own religious conversion occurred at this juncture. In support of the state religion he wrote several poems in praise of Apollo, Diana, Mercury, and other tutelary deities. Closely associated with the poems of this period are the odes included in the section called The Golden Mean, which deplore the increase of wealth and luxury and urge his countrymen to imitate the virtuous uprightness of their ancestors.

As the leading poet of Rome Horace wrote the Secular Hymn in 17 B.C. and the Ode to Apollo (IV, 6) that describes the occasion for it. Among the later written odes of the fourth book, published in 13 B.C., are several in celebration of the successful military campaign prosecuted by the emperor's stepsons, Drusus and Tiberius, against the mountain tribes of the Alps. The book appropriately closes with an ode of thanksgiving for universal peace, addressed to Augustus. Horace had come all the way from idealistic loyalty to the Roman republic to fervid support of the imperial rule.

The Happy Isles

Epode 16

Scourges of civil dissension now lash us, the new generation,
   And Rome by her own strength is falling ruin-banned,
For whose overthrowing prevailed not her neighbors, the Marsian
      nation,
   Nor Tuscan Porsena with vainly threatening hand;

She whom Capua's rivalry could not destroy, neither Spartacus'
      daring,
   No, nor the Gallic rebel's doubly traitorous sword;
She who quailed not from Germany's brood with their blue eyes
      savagely glaring,
   Nor stooped to Hannibal by mothers all-abhorred:—

Rome her unnatural sons blood-tainted to ruin are bringing:
   Wild beasts again for lairs shall choose the soil of Rome:
Aliens triumphant shall trample her ashes: with hoof-strokes
      ringing
   The horsemen of our foes shall spurn the ancient home.

And the bones of Quirinus, from wind and from sun covered close
      through the ages,
   Shall be—oh sight accurst!—flung wide with brutal laugh.
Where shall a haven be found from the tempest around us that
      rages,
   Seek ye, my countrymen?—or ye, their nobler half?

Let this be our counsel of counsels:—as when, after dread oath
      taken,
   The people of Phocaea left their Asian home,

Fled from their lands, from the hearths of their fathers, their tem-
ples, forsaken
For boars to dwell therein, for ravening wolves to roam:—

Let us go, whither fortune may guide, whither over the surges the
finger
Of wild South-west or West wind beckons us away.
Thus are ye minded? Hath any aught better to counsel? Why linger
To haste aboard the ship in this the accepted day?

But first let us swear—"When stones from the depths of the sea
up-swimming
Return, be our return forfended by no ban;
And let not our consciences smite us, as homeward-bound we are
trimming
The sails, when Po shall lave hill-crests Apulian;

When towering out of the sea rise Apennine's forest battalions;
When love unnatural shall in monstrous bonds unite
Beast unto beast, when the stag with the tigress shall wanton in
dalliance,
And when the dove shall take for paramour the kite;

When the herds shall be trustful, their dread of the tawny lion
have vanished,
And goats shall gleam in scales, and love the briny sea."
Take we these oaths, yea, all by which hope of return shall be
banished,
Then one and all go forth, an exiled nation we—

Or all save the dullard mob: the fearful and unbelieving
May still, a craven rout, on beds unhallowed lie.
Ye, who have hearts heroic, away with unmanly grieving!
Aboard! with woven wings by shores Etruscan fly!

Us Ocean awaiteth, the girdler of earth: let us seek, on-sailing,
The fields of Paradise, the Islands of the Blest,

Where yearly the soil without tillage bestoweth the harvests un-
     failing,
Where blossoms aye the vine by pruner's knife undressed.

The olive shoot burgeons, the husbandman's trust it betrayeth
     never:
Dark-emerald figs begem the trees ungrafted there:
Out of the holm-oak's hollow the gold of the comb drips ever:
With tinkling foot the rill leaps down its mountain stair.

There to the pails unbidden the milch-goats come in the gloaming:
For love the heifer comes full-uddered to the byre.
They fear not at even the growl of the bear round the sheepfold
     roaming;
Nor earth with viper-nests swells up in hillocks dire:

No murrain e'er blasteth the flock, no dog-star fierily-gleaming
Beats on the herd, with fury parching every vein.
Yea, in blissful surprise shall we note how never the waterfloods,
     streaming
From clouds the East-wind chases, scourge the sodden plain:
Nor there mid the dry clods parched are the seeds, once fatness-
     teeming;
For still the King of Heaven there tempers sun and rain.

Hitherward rowed by her heroes never came Argo racing;
The shameless dame of Colchis never trod its strand:
Never shipman of Sidon came hither, their yards on the new tack
     bracing:
Ulysses' toil-worn crew ne'er touched at that blest land.

Jupiter veiled those shores, and reserved for a godfearing nation,
When he with brass-alloy debased the Age of Gold—
With brass: but with iron yet harder his wrath made each genera-
     tion:
The way to 'scape wherefrom my prophet-lips have told.

Arthur S. Way

Civil War

Epode 7

Why do ye rush, oh wicked folk,
   To a fresh war?
Again the cries, the sword, the smoke—
   What for?

Has not sufficient precious blood
   Been fiercely shed?
Must ye spill more until ye flood
   The dead?

Not even armed in rivalry
   Your hate's employed;
But 'gainst yourselves until ye be
   Destroyed!

Even when beasts slay beasts, they kill
   Some other kind.
Can it be madness makes ye still
   So blind?

Make answer! Is your conscience numb?
   Each ashy face
Admits, with silent lips, the dumb
   Disgrace.

Murder of brothers! Of all crime,
   Vilest and worst!
Pause—lest ye be, through all of time,
   Accursed.

Louis Untermeyer

The Ship of State

Odes I, 14

O Ship! new billows sweep thee out
Seaward. What wilt thou? hold the port, be stout.
  Seest not? thy mast
How rent by stiff south-western blast,

Thy side, of rowers how forlorn?
Thine hull, with groaning yards, with rigging torn,
    Can ill sustain
  The fierce, and ever fiercer main;

Thy gods, no more than sails entire,
From whom yet once thy need might aid require.
    O Pontic pine,
  The first of woodland stocks is thine,

Yet race and name are but as dust.
Not painted sterns give storm-tost seamen trust,
    Unless thou dare
  To be the sport of storms, beware.

Of old at best a weary weight,
A yearning care and constant strain of late,
    O shun the seas
  That gird those glittering Cyclades.

W. E. Gladstone

Before Actium

Epode 1

While you, Maecenas, dearest friend,
    Would Caesar's person with your own defend;
      And Antony's high-tower'd fleet,
With light Liburnian galleys fearless meet,
      What shall forsaken Horace do,
Whose every joy of life depends on you?
      With thee, 'tis happiness to live,
And life, without thee, can no pleasure give.
      Shall I th' unkind command obey,
And idly waste my joyless hours away;
      Or, as becomes the brave, embrace
The glorious toil, and spurn the thoughts of peace?
      I will; and over Alpine snow,
Or savage Caucasus intrepid go;
      Or follow with undaunted breast
Thy dreadful warfare to the farthest west.
      You ask, what aid I can afford,
A puny warrior, novice to the sword:
      Absence, my lord, increases fear;
The danger lessens when the friend is near:
      Thus, if the mother-bird forsake
Her unfledged young, she dreads the gliding snake,
      With deeper agonies afraid,
Not that her presence could afford them aid.
      With cheerful heart will I sustain,
To purchase your esteem, this dread campaign:
      Not that my ploughs, with heavier toil,
Or with a larger team, may turn my soil;
      Not that my flocks, when Sirius reigns,
May browse the verdure of Lucania's plains;
      Not that my villa shall extend
To where the walls of Tusculum ascend.

Thy bounty largely hath supplied,
Even with a lavish hand, my utmost pride;
    Nor will I meanly wish for more,
Tasteless in earth to hide the sordid store,
        Like an old miser in the play,
Or like a spendthrift squander it away.

Philip Francis

At the Battle

Epode 9

O when, Maecenas, happy friend, shall I,
        At Caesar's victory elated,
Drink with you 'neath your stately dome—please Jove!—
    The Caecuban that long has waited

A festal banquet, while the strains alternate
    Of foreign pipes and Doric lyre—
As late when fled the captain, son of Neptune,
    Driven from the sea, his fleet afire,

He that had threatened Rome with chains he'd struck
    From perjured slaves in friendly act.
The Roman soldier, made a woman's chattel—
    Posterity, ye'll scout the fact!—

Yet carries arms and stakes, and can endure
    Even wrinkled eunuchs to obey,
And mid the military standards—shame!—
    Mosquito curtains flaunt the day.

And yet two thousand Galli, shouting "Caesar!"
    On snorting horses sought our side,
And all the hostile navy, bearing leftwards,
    Make for port and hidden bide.

Hail, god of Triumph! Why delay to bring
    White bulls ne'er yoked and golden cars?
Hail, god of Triumph! Such a general back
    Thou brought'st not from Jugurthine wars,

Nor Africanus such, whose monument
    Valour on ruined Carthage raised.
The foe, subdued on sea and land, has changed
    His purple cloak for black, amazed:

Either he makes for hundred-citied Crete
    Though winds unfavourable be,
Or seeks the Syrtes by the south wind harassed,
    Or vaguely drifts upon the sea.

Here, boy; come, bring us more capacious bowls,
    And Chian bring and Lesbian wine;
Or duly mix for us the Caecuban,
    To check those rising qualms of mine.

For all my fears for Caesar's fortunes, sure
Than sweet Lyaeus there's no better cure.

Alexander Falconer Murison

The Death of Cleopatra

Odes I, 37

Now, comrades, 'tis the hour
    To quaff the wine and with swift dancing feet
Disdain the ground in joyous measures meet:
    It was full time to dower
The couches of the gods and grateful bring
    Gifts for their banqueting.

But impious it had been
From cellars old the Caecuban to draw
In the dark days when panic-struck we saw
Aghast the frenzied queen
With threats of ruin, arrogant in soul
Menace the Capitol.

She with wild hope elate,
'Mid the foul crew that did her company,
Drunken with Fortune's smile had thought to be
The favourite aye of Fate;
But scarce one galley saved from burning fire
Minished her fury dire.

Not Mareotic then
Her mind to soaring dreams insensate wrought,
While grim reality great Caesar brought
To tame that ardour when
He pressed upon her as she turned to flee
Fearful from Italy.

As hawk that swift of flight
Stoops o'er the dove or on Thessalian snows
The hunter on the flying hare will close,
So Caesar in his might
That fateful portent as she timorous fled
With chains swift followéd.

Then she in nobler wise
Seeking to perish quailed not at the sword,
In woman fashion nor the gods implored
To show her fainting eyes
Some secret shore of safety o'er the main
Her galley swift might gain.

With countenance serene
She visited her fallen house, and brave
Took in her hands the serpents fierce they gave,

With calm untroubled mien;
Pressing the poisoned fangs unto her side
    As bridegroom would a bride.

Her soul exultantly
Rose at the thought that such a death could bring
Contempt and scorn on that proud triumphing,
    And fierce Ligurians see
No crownless queen with veiléd eyes advance
    To grace their arrogance.

A. L. Taylor

Augustus, Guardian of Rome

Odes I, 2

Since Jove decreed in storms to vent
    The winter of his discontent,
Thundering o'er Rome impenitent
    With red right hand,
The flood-gates of the firmament
    Have drenched the land!

Terror hath seized the minds of men,
Who deemed the days had come again
When Proteus led, up mount and glen,
    And verdant lawn,
Of teeming ocean's darksome den
    The monstrous spawn.

When Pyrrha saw the ringdove's nest
Harbour a strange unbidden guest,
And, by the deluge dispossest

Of glade and grove
Deers down the tide, with antler'd crest,
    Affrighted drove.

We saw the yellow Tiber, sped
Back to his Tuscan fountain-head,
O'erwhelm the sacred and the dead
    In one fell doom,
And Vesta's pile in ruins spread,
    And Numa's tomb.

Dreaming of days that once had been,
He deemed that wild disastrous scene
Might soothe his Ilia, injured queen!
    And comfort give her,
Reckless though Jove should intervene,
    Uxorious river!

Our sons will ask, why men of Rome
Drew against kindred, friends, and home,
Swords that a Persian hecatomb
    Might best imbue—
Sons, by their fathers' feuds become
    Feeble and few!

Whom can our country call in aid?
Where must the patriot's vow be paid?
With orisons shall vestal maid
    Fatigue the skies?
Or will not Vesta's frown upbraid
    Her votaries?

Augur Apollo! shall we kneel
To *thee,* and for our commonweal
With humbled consciousness appeal?
    Oh, quell the storm!
Come, though a silver vapour veil
    Thy radiant form!

Will Venus from Mount Eryx stoop,
And to our succour hie, with troop
Of laughing Graces, and a group
    Of Cupids round her?
Or comest *thou* with wild war-whoop,
    Dread Mars! our founder?

Whose voice so long bade peace avaunt;
Whose war-dogs still for slaughter pant;
The tented field thy chosen haunt,
    Thy child the Roman,
Fierce legioner, whose visage gaunt
    Scowls on the foeman.

Or hath young Hermes, Maia's son,
The graceful guise and form put on
Of thee, Augustus? and begun
    (Celestial stranger!)
To wear the name which *thou* hast won—
    "Caesar's Avenger"?

Blest be the days of thy sojourn,
Distant the hour when Rome shall mourn
The fatal sight of thy return
    To Heaven again,
Forced by a guilty age to spurn
    The haunts of men.

Rather remain, beloved, adored,
Since Rome, reliant on thy sword,
To thee of Julius hath restored
    The rich reversion;
Baffle Assyria's hovering horde,
    And smite the Persian!

Francis Sylvester Mahony

The Poet's Conversion

Odes I, 34

I whom the Gods had found a client,
  Rarely with pious rites compliant,
At Unbelief disposed to nibble,
And pleased with every sophist quibble—
I, who had deemed great Jove a phantom,
Now own my errors, and recant 'em!

Have I not lived of late to witness,
Athwart a sky of passing brightness,
The God, upon his car of thunder,
Cleave the calm elements asunder?
And, through the firmament careering,
Level his bolts with aim unerring?

Then trembled Earth with sudden shiver;
Then quaked with fear each mount and river;
Stunned at the blow, Hell reeled a minute,
With all the darksome caves within it;
And Atlas seemed as he would totter
Beneath his load of land and water!

Yes! of a God I hail the guidance;
The proud are humbled at his biddance;
Fortune, his handmaid, now uplifting
Monarchs, and now the sceptre shifting,
With equal proof his power evinces,
Whether she raise or ruin Princes.

Francis Sylvester Mahony

To Apollo and Diana

Odes I, 21

Virgins, sing the Virgin Huntress;
    Youths, the youthful Phoebus sing;
Sing Latona, she who bore them
    Dearest to the eternal King:
Sing the heavenly maid who roves
Joyous, through the mountain groves;
She who winding waters loves;
    Let her haunts her praises ring!

Sing the vale of Peneus' river;
    Sing the Delian deity;
The shoulder glorious with its quiver;
    And the Lyre of Mercury.
From our country, at our prayer—
Famine, plague, and tearful war
These, benign, shall drive afar
    To Persia's plains or Britain's sea.

Patrick Branwell Brontë

Light-Footed and Light-Fingered Mercury

Odes I, 10

Mercury! Atlas' smooth-tongued boy, whose will
    First trained to speech our wildest, earliest race,
And gave their rough-hewn forms with supple skill
    The gymnast's grace.

Be it my task thy glories to declare,
Herald of Jove! inventor of the lyre;
Right apt in merry theft to take whate'er
    Thou may'st desire.

When as a boy the oxen stolen by thee,
He urged thee to restore, light-fingered one!
Chiding Apollo turned and laughed to see
    His quiver gone.

Rich-laden Priam, by thy favour led
Amid the foe beneath the encompassed wall,
Through sentries and Thessalian watch-fires sped
    Unseen by all.

'Tis thine the unbodied spirits of the blessed
To guide to bliss, and with thy golden rod
To rule the shades; above, below, caressed
    By every god.

                George John Whyte-Melville

Bacchus the Divine

Odes II, 19

I've watched (believe me, future years!)
    While Bacchus taught the Nymphs a lay,
And goat-foot Satyrs pricked their ears,
    Over the mountains far away.

Hail, Bacchus, to thee! even now
    My heart's a-leap with joy and fright;
Hail and forbear! for dread art thou
    When thou dost lift thy rod to smite.

So may I praise thy devotees
  Who never tire, the founts of wine,
The honey-drip from hollow trees,
  The foaming streams of milk divine,

So sing how 'mid the stars is set
  The Crown of thy transfigured spouse,
The awful end Lycurgus met,
  The utter wreck of Pentheus' house.

Thou swayest streams and outer seas,
  And full of wine on some lone hill
Bindest the locks of Maenades
  In knots of vipers, scatheless still.

Once when the godless Giant gang
  Would put thy Father's realm to sack,
Armed with a lion's claw and fang
  Thou, thou didst topple Rhoetus back.

Men knew thy worth in dance and game
  And jesting, but did doubt thy part
In fight: yet wert thou still the same
  Alike of war and peace the heart.

Thee with thy golden horn bedecked
  E'en Cerberus grew mild to greet:
He brushed thee with his tail, and licked
  With all his tongues thy home-set feet.

                                        W. S. Marris

Bacchic Frenzy

Odes III, 25

Where dost thou drag me, son of Semele,
　　Me who am lost in wine?
Through what love-groves, through what wild haunts of thine
Am I, in this strange frenzy, forced to flee?
From what deep caverns (as I meditate
On peerless Caesar's fame and deathless fate)
Shall I be heard, when my exulting cries
Proclaim him friend of Jove, and star in yon bright skies?
Something I'll shout, new, strange, as yet unsung
　　By any other human tongue!

Thus, stung by thee, the sleepless Bacchanals ever
Grow mad whilst gazing on the Hebrus river,
On snow-white Thrace, and Rhodope, whose crown
　　Barbarian footsteps trample down.
　　And oh! like them it joys my soul
　　To wander where the rivers roll,
To gaze upon the dark and desert groves.

O thou great power, whom the Naiad loves
And Bacchant women worship (who o'erthrow
　　The mighty ash-trees as they go).
　　Nothing little, nothing low,
　　Nothing mortal, will I sing.
'Tis risk, but pleasant risk, O king,
To follow thus a god who loves to twine
His temples with the green and curling vine.

Bryan Waller Proctor

Ode to Fortune

Odes I, 35

O Lady Fortune! 'tis to thee I call,
　Dwelling at Antium, thou hast power to crown
The veriest clod with riches and renown,
　And change a triumph to a funeral.
The tillers of the soil and they that vex the seas,
Confessing thee supreme, on bended knees
　　Invoke thee, all.

Of Dacian tribes, of roving Scythian bands,
Of cities, nations, lawless tyrants red
With guiltless blood, art thou the haunting dread;
　Within thy path no human valor stands,
And, arbiter of empires, at thy frown
The sceptre, once supreme, slips surely down
　　From kingly hands.

Necessity precedes thee in thy way;
Hope fawns on thee, and Honor, too, is seen
Dancing attendance with obsequious mien;
　But with what coward and abject dismay
The faithless crowd and treacherous wantons fly
When once their jars of luscious wine run dry,—
　　Such ingrates they!

Fortune, I call on thee to bless
Our king,—our Caesar girt for foreign wars!
Help him to heal these fratricidal scars
　That speak degenerate shame and wickedness;
And forge anew our impious spears and swords,
Wherewith we may against barbarian hordes
　　Our Past redress!

Eugene Field

Gods and Heroes

Odes I, 12

W hat man, what hero, will you raise,
   By the shrill pipe, or deeper lyre!
What god, O Clio, will you praise,
   And teach the Echoes to admire?

Amidst the shades of Helicon,
   Cold Haemus' top, or Pindus' head,
Whence the glad forests hastened down,
   And danced as tuneful Orpheus played.

Taught by the muse, he stopped the fall
   Of rapid floods, and charmed the wind:
The listening oaks obeyed the call,
   And left their wondering hills behind.

Whom should I first record, but Jove,
   Whose sway extends o'er sea and land,
The king of men and gods above,
   Who holds the seasons in command?

To rival Jove, shall none aspire;
   None shall to equal glory rise;
But Pallas claims beneath her sire
   The second honours of the skies.

To thee, O Bacchus, great in war,
   To Dian will I strike the string,
Of Phoebus wounding from afar,
   In numbers like his own I'll sing.

The muse Alcides shall resound;
   The twins of Leda shall succeed;

This for the standing fight renowned,
　　And that for managing the steed,

Whose star shines innocently still:
　　The clouds disperse; the tempests cease;
The waves, obedient to their will,
　　Sink down, and hush their rage to peace.

Next shall I Numa's pious reign,
　　Or thine, O Romulus, relate;
Or Rome, by Brutus freed again;
　　Or haughty Cato's glorious fate?

Or dwell on noble Paulus' fame,
　　Too lavish of the patriot's blood?
Or Regulus' immortal name,
　　Too obstinately just and good?

These, with Camillus brave and bold,
　　And other chiefs of matchless might,
Rome's virtuous poverty of old
　　Severely seasoned to the fight.

Like trees, Marcellus' glory grows
　　With an insensible advance;
The Julian star, like Cynthia, glows,
　　Who leads the planetary dance.

The Fates, O sire of human race,
　　Intrust great Caesar to thy care;
Give him to hold thy second place,
　　And reign thy sole vicegerent here.

And whether India he shall tame,
　　Or to his chains the Seres doom;
Or mighty Parthia dreads his name,
　　And bows her haughty neck to Rome;

While on our groves thy bolts are hurled,
    And thy loud car shakes heaven above,
He shall with justice awe the world,
    To none inferior but to Jove.

Christopher Pitt

The Return of Augustus

Odes III, 14

O Commons, just as Hercules of yore,
    Tho' death should be the price, sought crowns of bay,
So conquering Caesar from the Spanish shore
    Comes home again today.

Since thou to righteous heaven hast proffered thanks,
    Come forth, O matron, faithful to thy spouse,
Our famous leader's sister, too, and ranks
    Of dames whose suppliant brows

Are circleted in gratitude to learn
    Of sons' and daughters' safety. I beseech
Ye, youths and maidens yet unwed, to spurn
    All unpropitious speech.

This truly festal day shall banish all
    My somber cares; while Caesar's mandates bend
The empire, I shall fear nor civil brawl
    Nor death by violent end.

Haste, boy, both balms and wreaths this day demands,
    Wine, too, whose date harks back to Marsian strife,
If aught, perchance, escaped when roving bands
    Of Spartacus were rife.

Then bid clear-voiced Neaera haste to tie
  In comely knot her wealth of chestnut hair,
But if her porter churl thy knock deny,
  Begone, nor tarry there.

A whitening head subdues the soul that long
  Inclined to spleen and quarrels' headstrong grip;
My fiery youth would not have brooked such wrong
  In Plancus' consulship.

Warren H. Cudworth

To Apollo

Odes IV, 6

Thou who the children of sad Niobe
    For the proud vaunt with vengeance visited,
Who the incontinent Tityus wrathfully
    Sent to a doom so dread!—

Phthian Achilles who in might surpassed
    The ranks of men and wellnigh to the ground
Brought the proud might of Ilion, at last
    No match for thee was found.

Yea, though Sea-Thetis owned him for her son,
    And though he made the Dardan towers to shake
With his terrific spear, ere victory won,
    Thy shafts could overtake.

Like pine that feels the biting axe's blow
    Or cypress bowed by Eurus' onset dread,
He fell, a giant form, and laid full low
    In Trojan dust his head.

That towering spirit ne'er had stooped to hide
    In steed that so Minerva's worship feigned;
The ignoble stratagem his soul of pride
    Had utterly disdained;

Disdained to steal like a nocturnal thief
    On Priam's halls with festal dances gay,
Turning that ill-timed Trojan mirth to grief,
    To gloom that holiday.

No, he had met his foes in open fight
    And ruthless laughed his captives' tears to scorn,
Their infants given to flames, O piteous sight,
    Nor spared the babe unborn,

Had not thy prayers, the prayers of Venus dear
    Moved mighty Jove to save from that distress,
That so Aeneas nobler walls might rear
    With surer auspices.

O thou who lavest in the Xanthus stream
    The locks divine that o'er thy shoulders flow—
The strains melodious that the Muse beseem
    On Thalia dost bestow!—

Defend the glory of the Daunian Muse,
    Breath of my song, to thee is due its fame,
The gift is thine that men no more refuse
    To me the poet's name.

Therefore ye maidens and ye youths who know
    Illustrious sires, to Delia still so dear,
The huntress-queen whose all-arresting bow
    The stags and lynxes fear,

See that ye keep the perfect Lydian time,
    And as my finger beats the measure true,
Of Leto's children sound in song sublime
    The praises that are due.

Apollo sing, ye youths, ye maidens fair
　　The growing crescent of the Queen of night,
Who makes the fields those golden harvests bear,
　　The moons so swift of flight.

So in the after-days when thou hast been
　　Long time a wedded wife thou shalt recall
In silent reverie the solemn scene
　　Of this high festival;

And as my songs fall soft upon thine ear,
　　Songs that the gods so love, then sung by thee,
Horatius' name shall once again be dear
　　For that fair memory.

A. L. Taylor

The Secular Hymn

*Written for the Secular Games
celebrated by Augustus in* 17 B.C.

O Phoebus, O Diana, forest Queen,
　　Ye glorious splendours of the sky,
Adored and evermore to be adored,
　　This sacred season hear our cry—

The season when the Sibyl's verse prescribed
　　That chosen maids and lads unstained
Should sing a hymn unto the gods whose favour
　　The seven hills ever have retained.

O fostering Sun, who in thy radiant car
　　Bring'st day and hid'st it in the tomb
And risest other yet the same, may'st thou
　　Ne'er look on greater thing than Rome.

Lucina, Ilithyia, Genitalis—
   Whichever name thou choose to bear—
Who gently bringst the babes to timely birth
   Hold mothers in thy special care.

O goddess, rear our offspring; prosper thou
   The wise decrees the Senate passed
Concerning wedlock and the marriage law
   To multiply the people fast,

So the full cycle, years ten times eleven,
   May bring again the games and songs
In clear day thrice and thrice in genial night,
   Presenting them to countless throngs.

And, Parcae, truthful in your past predictions,
   As once for all the promise stood—
And may the Empire's stablished landmark keep it!—
   Our future, like our past, make good.

Let Earth, producing fruits and flowers in plenty,
   Give Ceres wreaths of ears of corn,
And may salubrious rains and winds of heaven,
   Give nourishment to what is born.

Lay by thy bow, Apollo, mild and gentle,
   And lend the suppliant lads thine ear;
Thou, Luna, crescent Queen of starry heaven,
   Deign thou the suppliant maids to hear!

If Rome is work of yours, and Trojan bands
   In safety gained the Tuscan shore—
The remnant that you bade to change their homes
   And city, those for whom of yore

The chaste Aeneas, who survived his country,
   Through blazing Troy a way did find,
Unharmed, and destined to secure for them
   Yet more than what they left behind:

Ye gods, grant honest ways to docile youth,
  To placid age a tranquil bourn,
And to the Roman people wealth and children
  And all the gifts that life adorn!

The famous race of Venus and Anchises,
  With white steers praying, favour show;
Grant what they ask—a race that quell the fighter,
  Yet clement to the prostrate foe.

Now dread the Parthians the might of Rome
  By sea and land, her axes fear;
Now Scythians, lately haughty, send appeals,
  And Indian embassies come here.

Now Trust, Peace, Honour, ancient Modesty,
  And Virtue slighted and forlorn,
Take courage to return, and Plenty comes
  Rejoicing with her brimming horn.

If Phoebus, god of augury, resplendent
  With gleaming bow, dear to the Nine,
Phoebus, who by his healing art can soothe
  The wearied limbs of those that pine,

If he beholds the Palatine with favour,
  And Latium, and the Roman State,
May he preserve them yet another cycle,
  An age of ever happier fate!

And may Diana of the Aventine
  And Algidus the Fifteen hear,
And may she lend the prayers of the youth
  A gracious and attentive ear!

That Jove so wills it, yea, and all the gods,
  A good and sure hope home I bring—
I, Chorus, taught to sing Diana's praise,
  The praise of Phoebus taught to sing.

Alexander Falconer Murison

An Eagle of the Claudian Race

Odes IV, 4

Like a young eagle on the wing,
    Armed with the thunderbolt of Jove,
Made by the King of Gods the king
    Of all the feathered tribes that rove
The air,—his guerdon, as we read,
For capturing fair Ganymede,—

First, youth and native energy
    To untried labors fire his breast,—
We see the tender fledgling try
    A flight from the maternal nest;
Next, vernal winds and cloudless days
Invite him to more bold essays;

And yet a while, and grown more bold,
    Abroad by hostile impulse sent,
He swoops upon the shepherd fold;
    But now, on feast and fight intent,
He seizes serpents in their lair,
And wrestles with them in the air:

Thus Drusus waging war, they saw,—
    The mountaineer Vindelici,—
In Rhoetian Alps (but whence they draw
    The custom immemorially
Of carrying in their attacks
The Amazonian battle-axe

On their right arms, I'll not enquire,—
    For all things one ought not to know):
But when by youth's address and fire
    The conquerors of long ago
Are beaten in their turn, and feel
The force of his victorious steel,—

Thus bravely overthrown they find
  What nurture adds to nature's gifts;
That discipline, of heart and mind
  Alike, to nobler manhood lifts;
And heights to which the Neros grow
The training of Augustus show.

Brave men to gallant sires succeed;
  From good men are created good;
Lives in the steer and in the steed
  The virtue of ancestral blood;
Nor do ferocious eagles mate,
Unwarlike doves to generate.

Instruction a new force imparts
  To faculties inherited,
And, well directed, strengthens hearts
  In virtue's ways and valor's bred;
But when bad morals bring bad fame,
Good birth but aggravates the shame.

What thou, Rome, dost the Neros owe,
  The banks of the Metaurus tell,—
Where they first quelled the invading foe,
  And Hasdrubal defeated fell;
The sunlight of that brilliant day
Drove our Italian clouds away.

That smiling dawn of glory! when
  We first were victors, since in wrath
The African with mounted men
  Through Latium ploughed his bloody path,
As flame flies thro' pine forest trees
And east winds sweep Sicilian seas.

Thenceforth in deeds of high emprise
  The Roman youth have wrought and grown
In strength; restored, the temples rise,

In Punic tumults overthrown,—
And statues of the Gods again
Adorn the desecrated fane.

Then Hannibal, the faithless, said:
  "Deer, of rapacious wolves the prey,
We follow when we should have fled,—
  For do the best that do we may,
The greatest triumph we can know
Is to elude—escape our foe.

"Brave nation, that when Troy was burned,
  And in the ashes all seemed lost,
To other lands their faces turned,
  And, on the Tuscan billows tost,
Sons, aged sires, and Lares bore
To cities of the Ausonian shore.

"A race that,—like the black-leaved oak,
  The growth of fertile Algidus,
Shorn by the two-edged axe's stroke,—
  With a new strength repairs its loss;
In slaughter and defeat they feel
New courage bounding from the steel.

"A prodigy! and none so great
  Since Hercules the Hydra slew
When, as he lopped the monster's head,
  Straight from the wound another grew;
Or Jason's feat, or Cadmus' when
From dragon's teeth sprang armed men.

"Plunge it in depths profound,—it will
  Again with greater beauty rise;
Fight it,—and gloriously still
  The unscathed victor it defies,
And hostile legions puts to rout—
In battles wives will talk about.

"Couriers to Carthage, proud to spread
  News of my triumphs, I again
Shall never send,—for Fortune fled
  Our camp when Hasdrubal was slain;
Perished! the glories of our name,—
Perished! all hope of future fame."

There's nothing mortal that withstands
  The prowess of the Claudian race,
For Jove himself upholds their hands
  And clothes them with benignant grace,
While they, by care and counsel wise,
Above war's pangs and perils rise.

John Osborne Sargent

Prayer for Augustus

Odes IV, 5

Sprung from Gods, best guard of Rome,
  Long, too long, thou leav'st thy home.
Thou didst promise shorter stay;
Ah! return, the Fathers pray.

Ah! return, thy country cries,
Like the spring-time to our skies;
Days shall glide more sweetly o'er,
Suns come brighter to our shore.

As the mother mourns her son,
Who 'mid gales his course has run,
Forced Carpathian seas to roam,
Long a wanderer from sweet home—

How her prayers kind Heaven implore,
How she scans the winding shore—
So our hearts entreat the skies,
Rome for absent Caesar sighs.

Oxen safely roam the fields;
Ceres golden harvests yields;
Ships fly peaceful o'er the deep;
Faith and Truth their pledges keep.

Homes are pure, in virtue strong,
Law and order conquer wrong;
Gone the stain of former time,
Justice strikes the heels of crime.

Who the Scyth or Parthian fears,
Or the hordes Germania rears,
Or the wars with distant Spain?
Caesar lives—sweet peace shall reign.

Each the day of quiet sees;
Vines once more espouse the trees;
Swains return at evening hour;
Joyful they invoke thy power.

Prayer they offer, wine they pour,
Thee with household Gods adore;
Hercules thus Greece reveres;
Thus great Castor's name she fears.

Long thy reign, good Prince, we pray,
Grace by many a festal day;
This our prayer at sober morn,
This, at cheerful eve's return.

John B. Hague

Drusus and Tiberius

Odes IV, 14

What popular or what patrician care
        By carved inscriptions and memorial pages,
    Shall to the nations, through perpetual ages,
Thy name, Augustus, and thy virtues bear?

Greatest of princes thou, where'er the sun
    On habitable regions sheds a ray,
        Whom tribes that never knew the Latin sway
Know by late deeds of war so bravely done:

For gallant Drusus, with thy soldiery,
    Razed castles on tremendous Alpine heights,
        And routed more than once in bloody fights
The Breuni swift and fierce Vindelici;

While presently the elder Nero wages
    War with the savage Rhaetian mountaineers,
        And with imperial auspices appears
Conspicuous where the hottest battle rages;

Showing in mortal combats how to quell
    Men that would die rather than not be free;
        Victims to their wild love of liberty,
With wounds in front and face to heaven they fell.

And as the south wind tames the unbridled waves,
    And clouds are severed in the Pleiads' dances,
        Through paths of fire his uncurbed courser prances,
Where harried legions find their countless graves;

Or like the Aufidus that roaring flows,
    Bull-headed, through Apulian Daunus' realms,
        And in resistless fury overwhelms
The crop which on its well-tilled border grows:

Thus Claudius in impetuous onset rushed,
   The embattled legions cleft, nor lost a man;
   He strewed the field with corpses, rear and van,
And hordes of iron-clad barbarians crushed.

But thou the plans and forces didst provide,
   And thine the favoring gods, for on the day
   Abandoned Alexandria suppliant lay,
And ports and empty palace opened wide,

Propitious Fortune once more crowned thy arms
   In the third lustrum; and to thy commands,
   For victories achieved in other lands,
Awards renewing honors and fresh palms.

Till now untamed Cantabrians honor thee—
   Indians and nomad Scythians and the Medes—
   Whither our standards fly thy fame precedes,
Guard of Imperial Rome and Italy.

Thee doth the Danube, and mysterious Nile
   That hides its springs, obey; swift Tigris, thee;
   Thine appanage the monster-bearing sea
That rages round the Briton's distant isle!

Gallia, that faces death without a fear,
   Iberia, that our arms so long withstood,
   And the Sygambri who delight in blood—
Their weapons cast aside—thy name revere!

John Osborne Sargent

Thanksgiving for Peace

Odes IV, 15

When I to sing of battles dared aspire
  'Twas Phoebus who rebuked me with his lyre,
Lest I should launch upon th' Etruscan sea
With puny sails—Caesar, our heart's desire,

You brought rich harvests back to bless the land,
And gave again to Jove's protecting hand
  Those standards from the Parthian temples torn;
You, at the dawn of peace, have giv'n command

To close the Janus of Quirinus: you
Have bridled manners which from order due
  Had sunk to license, you rebuking sin
Have set us in the ancient ways anew,

Whereby the Latin race has won the name
Of strength and splendour, and that empire's fame
  Which stretches from the rising of the sun
Ev'n to the setting of his western flame.

No violence, while Caesar guards the state,
Shall drive away our peace, nor mutual hate,
  Nor anger forging swords and whelming towns
In civil bloodshed's miserable fate.

Not those who drink the Danube, nor Chinese,
Getae nor Parthians, faithless enemies,
  Not those who dwell beside the Tanais
Will dare to break the Julian decrees.

We, both on days of work and holidays,
When to our lips the cheering cup we raise,
  With wives and children, as in duty bound,
Will give the gods their due of prayer and praise,

And, after, we shall hymn the men who played
The valiant part (with Lydian pipes to aid
   Our voices), Troy, Anchises and the race
Of gentle Venus, as our fathers bade.

Hugh MacNaghten

The Countryman

Virgil in his Georgics described and extolled the labors of the farm according to the ancient Roman pattern, but Horace is the poet of country life as it affects the spirit of man. "I live as my own master," he wrote to his intimate friend Aristius Fuscus, "when I have once left behind what you townsmen praise to the skies. Deliver me from all the works of greatness. Life in a poor cot is preferable to that of kings and their favorites."

His earliest poem on the pleasures of the country is a satirical sketch of the ingrained city man who dreams of leaving his business for the charming occupations of the farm, but when it comes to the point finds that he cannot tear himself away from the life to which he has grown accustomed.

Horace himself always emphasized relaxation when he spoke of his Sabine Farm. Except to advise a neighbor to plant nothing but the grape on his estate, he almost never referred in detail to the activities of agriculture. He remarked that the farmers around smiled when he attempted to work in his own fields. He was content to leave these tasks to his bailiff and the slaves. Enough for the poet to make the first snowfall on Mount Soracte an occasion for sitting by the fire with a good friend and a newly opened jar of wine. He hoped to spend his last years among the Tiburtine hills, or if not there then at lovely Tarentum on the south Italian coast. This is like saying that one expects to retire to Rye, New York, but will settle for a bungalow at Miami Beach.

Associated with the Sabine Farm was one of the three occasions when Horace nearly lost his life. He had escaped unharmed from battle and survived shipwreck on the coast of Sicily, only to miss death by a hair's breadth from a falling tree. He at once excoriated the ill-starred log in poetry, and at some later time he celebrated the anniversary of his lucky escape.

A charming group of five poems treats of rustic superstitions and rural festivals to the gods. A kid is to be sacrificed to the fountain of Bandusia, a boar to the pine tree sacred to Diana. The day of Faunus and the day of Neptune claim observance. A farmer's daughter is assured that her offering of meal and salt is as acceptable to the gods as whole hecatombs of sheep, if given with pure hands and true devotion. This group probably comes nearer the heart of Horace's religion than do his official poems to the gods of the state.

The moderation that Horace found consonant with nature was more readily practiced at the Sabine Farm than at Rome. Hence his constant preference for life in a country setting.

The City Farmer

Epode 2

How happy in his low degree,
    How rich in humble Poverty, is he,
Who leads a quiet country life!
Discharg'd of business, void of strife,
And from the gripeing Scrivener free.
(Thus, e're the Seeds of Vice were sown,
    Liv'd Men in better Ages born,
Who Plow'd, with Oxen of their own,
    Their small paternal field of Corn.)
Nor Trumpets summon him to War
    Nor drums disturb his morning Sleep,
Nor knows he Merchants gainful care,
    Nor fears the dangers of the deep.
The clamours of contentious Law,
    And Court and state, he wisely shuns,
Nor brib'd with hopes, nor dar'd with awe,
    To servile Salutations runs;
But either to the clasping Vine
    Does the supporting Poplar Wed,
Or with his pruneing hook disjoyn
    Unbearing Branches from their Head,
    And grafts more happy in their stead:
Or climbing to a hilly steep,
    He views his Herds in Vales afar,
Or Sheers his overburden'd Sheep,
    Or mead for cooling drink prepares
    Of Virgin honey in the Jars.
Or in the now declining year,
    When bounteous *Autumn* rears his head,

63

He joyes to pull the ripen'd Pear,
   And clustring Grapes with purple spread.
The fairest of his fruit he serves,
   Priapus thy rewards:
Sylvanus too his part deserves,
   Whose care the fences guards.
Sometimes beneath an ancient Oak,
   Or on the matted grass he lies:
No God of Sleep he need invoke;
   The stream, that o're the pebbles flies,
   With gentle slumber crowns his Eyes.
The Wind, that Whistles through the sprays,
   Maintains the consort of the Song;
And hidden Birds, with native layes,
   The golden sleep prolong.
But when the blast of Winter blows,
   And hoary frost inverts the year,
Into the naked Woods he goes,
   And seeks the tusky Boar to rear,
   With well mouth'd hounds and pointed Spear.
Or spreads his subtile Nets from sight
   With twinckling glasses to betray
The Larkes that in the Meshes light,
   Or makes the fearful Hare his prey.
Amidst his harmless easie joys
   No anxious care invades his health,
Nor Love his peace of mind destroys,
   Nor wicked avarice of Wealth.
But if a chast and pleasing Wife,
To ease the business of his Life,
Divides with him his household care,
Such as the Sabine *Matrons* were,
Such as the swift *Apulians* Bride,
   Sunburnt and Swarthy tho' she be,
Will fire for Winter Nights provide,
   And without noise will oversee
   His Children and his Family,
And order all things till he come,

Sweaty and overlabour'd, home;
If she in pens his Flocks will fold,
   And then produce her Dairy store,
With Wine to drive away the cold,
   And unbought dainties of the poor;
Not Oysters of the *Lucrine* Lake
   My sober appetite wou'd wish,
   Nor *Turbet,* or the Foreign Fish
That rowling Tempests overtake,
   And hither waft the costly dish.
Not *Heathpout,* or the rarer Bird,
   Which *Phasis,* or *Ionia* yields,
More pleasing morsels wou'd afford
   Than the fat Olives of my fields;
Than Shards or Mallows for the pot,
   That keep the loosen'd Body sound
Or than the Lamb, that falls by Lot,
   To the just Guardian of my ground.
Amidst these feasts of happy Swains,
   The jolly Shepheard smiles to see
His flock returning from the Plains;
   The farmer is as pleas'd as he,
To view his Oxen, sweating smoak,
Bear on their Necks the loosen'd Yoke:
To look upon his menial Crew,
   That sit around his cheerful hearth,
And bodies spent in toil renew
   With wholesome Food and Country Mirth.

This *Morecraft* said within himself;
   Resolv'd to leave the wicked Town;
   And live retir'd upon his own;
He call'd his Mony in:
   But the prevailing love of pelf
   Soon split him on the former shelf,
And put it out again.

John Dryden

A Winter Party

Odes I, 9

O yonder see how clearly gleams
　　Soracte, white with snow;
How the forest labors beneath its load,
　　Bowing to let it go;
And the streamlets, numbed by the piercing cold,
　　At length have ceased to flow.

Dissolve the rigor of the frost,
　　Bright let the embers shine,
With liberal hand heap on the logs,
　　And, Thaliarchus mine,
Bring forth the Sabine amphora
　　Of four-years-mellowed wine.

All else abandon to the gods;
　　Whatever time they will
They drive the winds from the tossing sea
　　And cause them to be still,
Till never a lowland cypress stirs
　　Nor old ash on the hill.

Pry not into the morrow's store;
　　Thy profit doth advance
By every day that fate allots,
　　So, lad, improve thy chance,—
Ere stiff old age replace thy youth,—
　　To love and tread the dance.

Now in the Campus and the squares
　　At the appointed hour
Let gentle whispers oft be heard
　　From many a twilight bower,
Or the laugh of a lurking lass betray
　　The pledge of a ring or flower.

George F. Whicher

Northern Exposure

Odes I, 9

Look up to Pentland's tow'ring top,
    Buried beneath great wreaths of snaw,
O'er ilka cleugh, ilk scar, and slap,
    As high as ony Roman wa'.

Driving their baws frae whins or tee,
    There's noo nae gowfer to be seen,
Nor dousser fowk wysing a-jee
    The byast bouls on Tamson's green.

Then fling on coals, and ripe the ribs,
    And beek the house baith but and ben,
That mutchkin stoup it hauds but dribs,
    Then let's get in the tappit hen.

Good claret best keeps out the cauld,
    And drives away the winter soon;
It makes a man baith gash and bauld,
    And heaves his saul beyond the moon.

Leave to the gods your ilka care,
    If that they think us worth their while,
They can a' rowth of blessings spare,
    Which will our fasheous fears beguile.

For what they have a mind to do,
    That will they do, should we gang wood;
If they command the storms to blaw,
    Then upo' sight the hailstains thud.

But soon as e'er they cry, "Be quiet,"
    The blatt'ring winds dare nae mair move,
But cour into their caves, and wait
    The high command of supreme Jove.

Let neist day come as it thinks fit,
    The present minute's only ours;
On pleasure let's employ our wit,
    And laugh at fortune's feckless powers.

Be sure ye dinna quat the grip
    Of ilka joy when ye are young,
Before auld age your vitals nip,
    And lay ye twafald o'er a rung.

Sweet youth's a blyth and heartsome time;
    Then, lads and lasses, while it's May,
Gae pou the gowan in its prime,
    Before it wither and decay.

Watch the saft minutes of delyte,
    When Jenny speaks beneath her breath,
And kisses, laying a' the wyte
    On you, if she keap ony skaith.

"Haith, ye're ill-bred," she'll smiling say,
    "Ye'll worry me, you greedy rook";
Syne frae your arms she'll rin away,
    And hide hersell in some dark nook.

Her laugh will lead you to the place
    Where lies the happiness you want,
And plainly tells you to your face,
    Nineteen nay-says are haff a grant.

Now to her heaving bosom cling,
    And sweetly toolie for a kiss,
Frae her fair finger whop a ring,
    As taiken of a future bliss.

These bennisons, I'm very sure,
    Are of the gods' indulgent grant;
Then, surly carles, whisht, forbear,
    To plague us with your whining cant.

Allan Ramsay

Retirement

Odes II, 6

I'm sure, Septimius, thou wouldst go
    To Cadiz with me or explore
The haunts of our unconquered foe
    That dwell on the Cantabrian shore,—
And journey on to Afric lands
Through boiling waves and burning sands.

Worn as I am with war's alarms,
    Hard perils, and the billows' rage,—
Let me in Tibur's rural charms
    Find a calm haven for my age:
Some colonists of Grecian race
Were the first settlers of the place.

But should the Fates this boon deny,
    Tarentum is my second choice;
On sweet Galaesus' banks would I
    Amid the pastured flocks rejoice,
Whose fleeces show the shepherds' care
In the protecting skins they wear.

No spot on earth, where'er it lies,
    For me has such a power to please:
It beams with smiles, its honey vies
    With that of the Hymettian bees,
And green Venafrum cannot show
A field where finer olives grow.

The Springs are long, we breathe an air
    Moistened with warm and genial rains;
Flowers and fruits will flourish there,
    And vineyards pay the peasant's pains:
On hills hard by a wine is prest
That's equal to Falernum's best.

In that serene and happy seat,
　　Remote from worldly toil and strife,
Wilt thou with me in calm retreat
　　Tread the descending path of life,—
Till thou, bereaved, with tears regard
The ashes of thy friend the bard.

John Osborne Sargent

Come Home to Tibur

Odes I, 7

Let others hymn the glories of Rhodes or Mytilene,
　　Ephesus the golden, or Tempe, Thessaly's pride,
Battlemented Corinth on twin seas pillioned,
　　Delphi by Apollo, Thebes by Bacchus dignified.
Some never cease inditing of virgin Pallas' city,
　　Plucking all its olive-leaves to twine their singing-crowns;
Some to honor Juno vaunt the cavalcades of Argos,
　　Some Mycenae, wealthiest of the Grecian towns.
I would never tune a string for hardy Lacedaemon,
　　Never turn a stave for Larissa's bounteous loam;
Only let me sweetly sing Albunea's echoing cavern,
　　And the rocks where Anio leaps down in sudden foam,
Only praise through all my days the grove of old Tiburnus,
　　Where between the apple trees the lightfoot rillets roam.

Plancus, leave the pennon'd camp, come home to woody Tibur,
　　And as the white South Wind of Spring at last withholds his rain
And wipes the dusky clouds away, forget your weary labours
　　Over a bowl of mellow wine, that routs dull care and pain.
When Teucer put his angered sire and Salamis behind him,
　　'Tis told that with a poplar wreath he crowned his beaded brow
Glowing with heady fumes of sorrow-easing Bacchus,
　　And thus bespake his troubled friends, clustered round the prow:

"Whithersoever Fortune lead us, kinder than a father,
 Fellows and companions, together we will sail.
Dream not of despairing, while Teucer guards and guides you,
 Trusting in Apollo, whose promise cannot fail.
To a new land he calls us, to build another Salamis—
 Great-heart comrades, you and I have shared worse ills than these;
Fill with wine your cups and mine, tonight we drown our bodings,
 Then tomorrow forth once more over the vasty seas."

Edward Marsh

An American Paraphrase

Odes I, 7

*A Fragment Imitated
Addressed to Richard Howell, Esq., of
New Jersey, late Major in the Army.*

Let other bards, in sonorous, lofty song,
 Rehearse the glories of *European* climes;
The charms of *Britain* rapturously prolong,
 Of fam'd *Ierne* in heroic rhimes:—

Tell of *New-York*, on ev'ry side begirt,
 With *Hudson's* bleak, tempestuous, briny wave:
Of *Ab'ram's Plains* their tuneful powers exert,
 The fall of hero's and of vet'rans brave.

Of *Kent*, far distant, with a *farmer* blest,
 Whose Muse, oppression's out-stretch'd canvas furl'd;
Of *Pennsylvania*, happy in a *West*,
 The great Appelles of this infant world.

Some, praise *Madeira* for its gen'rous wine,
 And Schuylkill's pleasant shades and silver stream;
Or with pedantic pride, in strains divine,
 Dwell on the *Muses' Seat*,—their fav'rite theme.

Then with a feignéd patriotic zeal,
   Affect the soldier, and Virginia praise,—
Fam'd for her steeds; while some the public weal
   Of *Penn* in adulating numbers raise.

Nor *Boston's* police, or the high ting'd bowers
   Of fertile *Hampstead*, please so much, as where
The silver *Christiana* gently pours,
   A wat'ry tribute to the *Delaware*.

Where *Swanwick's* lofty trees, their summits raise,
   And fragrant orchards court the solar beam;
Pleas'd with the sight the waterman delays,
   To view the forest, dancing on the stream.

Surrounded by a verdant grove-fring'd mead,
   Which from the northern blasts its beauty shrouds,
N—— C——e seems to rear its antient head,
   And point its lustre to the passing clouds.

There may I live, inemulous of fame,
   Nor wish the laurel, or the poet's bays:
I ask not riches, or a mighty name,
   But there, in sweet content, to end my days.

John Parke

The Virtues of the Vine

Odes I, 18

In the rich fields of Tibur, Varus mine,
   Plant me no tree saving the sacred vine.
Be sober! and the gods will thwart your will.
Drink! and they rid you of the thoughts that kill.
Drink! and where's want or war? Thee, Bacchus, thee

We sing, thou lord of wine and jollity,
And Lady Venus, Queen of loveliness.
But lest thy temperate bounties man transgress,
They tell how long ago the bridal rout
Of Centaurs and of Lapiths fought it out,
Till all the board with wine and blood ran red,
And how thine hand is heavy on the head
Of Thracians, till they know not right nor wrong,
When reason quails, and hate and lust are strong.
For me, bright god, I bow me to thy will,
Nor dare to wake thee when thou wouldst be still,
Nor drag to light thy mysteries, unseen
Beneath their leafy shroud of dappled green.
Only do thou make mute the madding drum,
And bid the Berecynthian horn be dumb.
For in their train Self-love stone-blind doth tread,
Vain-glory lifting up her empty head,
And Faith that of a secret takes no heed,
False Faith, whose thoughts as in a glass men read.

Anonymous

Accursed Tree

Odes II, 13

Shame of thy mother soyle! ill-nurtur'd tree!
  Sett to the mischeife of posteritie!
That hand, (what 'ere it were) that was thy nurse,
Was sacrilegious, (sure) or somewhat worse.
Black, as the day was dismall, in whose sight
Thy rising topp first staind the bashfull light.
That man (I thinke) wrested the feeble life
From his old father. that man's barbarous knife
Conspir'd with darknes 'gainst the strangers throate;
(Whereof the blushing walles tooke bloody note)

Huge high-floune poysons, eu'n of Colchos breed,
And whatsoe're wild sinnes black thoughts doe feed,
His hands haue padled in; his hands, that found
Thy traiterous root a dwelling in my ground.
Perfidious totterer! longing for the staines
Of thy kind Master's well-deseruing braines.
Mans daintiest care, & caution cannot spy
The subtile point of his coy destiny,
Wch way it threats. With feare the merchants mind
Is plough'd as deepe, as is the sea with wind,
(Rowz'd in an angry tempest); Oh the sea!
Oh! that's his feare; there flotes his destiny:
While from another (unseene) corner blowes
The storme of fate, to wch his life he owes.
By Parthians bow the soldjer lookes to die,
(Whose hands are fighting, while their feet doe flie.)
The Parthian starts at Rome's imperiall name,
Fledg'd with her Eagles wing; the very chaine
Of his captivity rings in his eares.
Thus, o thus fondly doe wee pitch our feares
Farr distant from our fates. our fates, that mocke
Our giddy feares with an unlook't for shocke.

A little more, & I had surely seene
Thy greisly Majesty, Hell's blackest Queene;
And Aeacus on his Tribunall too,
Sifting the soules of guilt; & you, (oh you!)
You euer-blushing meads, where doe the Blest
Farr from darke horrors home appeale to rest.
There amorous Sappho plaines upon her Lute
Her loues crosse fortune, that the sad dispute
Runnes murmuring on the strings. Alcaeus there
In high-built numbers wakes his golden lyre,
To tell the world, how hard the matter went,
How hard by sea, by warre, by banishment.
There these braue soules deale to each wondring eare
Such words, soe precious, as they may not weare
Without religious silence; aboue all

Warres ratling tumults, or some tyrants fall.
The thronging clotted multitude doth feast.
What wonder? when the hundred-headed beast
Hangs his black lugges, stroakt with those heavenly lines;
The Furies curl'd snakes meet in gentle twines,
And stretch their cold limbes in a pleasing fire.
Prometheus selfe, & Pelops sterved Sire
Are cheated of their paines; Orion thinkes
Of Lions now noe more, or spotted Linx.

Richard Crashaw

A Narrow Escape

Odes II, 13

He reckoned his Arbor Day Friday,
    The thirteenth at that, I'll be bound;
At no sort of sacrilege shied he
    Who planted you here in my ground.

Who was it, old stump? Some assassin,
    Who knifed one he'd saved from a wreck,
Or caused his old granddad to pass in
    His checks by a twist of his neck?

Some heathen concocter of magic
    Set up this infernal machine,
And timed it, with irony tragic,
    To fall on mine innocent bean.

Us humans can never be certain,
    Though we try to sift fancy from fact,
What hour Fate may ring down the curtain
    On our poor little vaudeville act.

No use to stay home, with the notion
    That Neptune will spare you his wrath;
You miss a cold grave in the ocean,
    And slip on the soap in the bath.

Dodge War, lest a bullet may dent you—
    A splinter will land in your eye,
Or a brick from a chimney present you
    A pass to the Sweet By and By.

Orb *me*, how I missed by an eyebrow
    A bid to Proserpina's tea,
Where Alcaeus and Sappho the highbrow
    Give matinée concerts at three.

I almost heard Cerberus baying,
    And witnessed poor Tantalus' toils,
And gazed on the Furies, displaying
    The latest in serpentine coils.

Some sight! Just imagine it, can't you?
    Old Orion the hunter to boot.
I'd like to have seen 'em, I grant you,
    But I don't like the single track route.

Charles Ernest Bennett

To the Fountain of Bandusia

Odes III, 13

O fountain of Bandusia!
    Whence crystal waters flow,
With garlands gay and wine I'll pay
    The sacrifice I owe;

A sportive kid with budding horns
   I have, whose crimson blood
Anon shall dye and sanctify
   Thy cool and babbling flood.

O fountain of Bandusia!
   The Dog-star's hateful spell
No evil brings into the springs
   That from thy bosom well;
Here oxen, wearied by the plough,
   The roving cattle here
Hasten in quest of certain rest,
   And quaff thy gracious cheer.

O fountain of Bandusia!
   Ennobled shalt thou be,
For I shall sing the joys that spring
   Beneath yon ilex-tree.
Yes, fountain of Bandusia,
   Posterity shall know
The cooling brooks that from thy nooks
   Singing and dancing go.

Eugene Field

Fontinalia

Odes III, 13

Bandusian fountain! worthy of sweet wine
   Nor lacking garlands strewn, thy glassy stream;
To-morrow from the frolic herd I deem
The tenderest kid of any shall be thine.
His pulsing blood shall tinge thy crystalline
   Cold water, though by budding front he seem
   Destined to wax in love and war supreme:
But vain his destiny. To weary kine

And wandering flocks thy runnel, icy cool,
  Gives grateful rest when flaming Sirius reigns.
  Among the founts in noble numbers known
Thou too shalt be exalted, while my strains
  Extol the rills, from ledges ilex-grown,
  That murmuring fill thy pure pellucid pool.

George F. Whicher

For Diana's Pine

Odes III, 22

O Virgin Warder of the mountain pines!
    On whom, in sorrow, matrons not in vain
Thrice call, and Thou dost quell their every pain,—
  Three-fold Thy God-head shines!

  Close to my roof let this Thy pine tree grow,
On which, as each revolving year is o'er
Gladly from some fierce, sideward-thrusting boar
  Blood-offering I'll bestow.

George Meason Whicher

To a Faun

Odes III, 18

Wooer of young Nymphs who fly thee,
    Lightly o'er my sunlit lawn,
Trip, and go, nor injured by thee
  Be my weanling herds, O Faun:

If the kid his doomed head bows, and
    Brims with wine the loving cup,
When the year is full; and thousand
    Scents from altars hoar go up.

Each flock in the rich grass gambols
    When the month comes which is thine;
And the happy village rambles
    Fieldward with the idle kine:

Lambs play on, the wolf their neighbour:
    Wild woods deck thee with their spoil;
And with glee the sons of labour
    Stamp upon their foe the soil.

Charles Stuart Calverley

Hymn for the Neptunalia

Odes III, 28

What better do this day
    Of Neptune, Lyde, say,
Than broach the cask
Of Caecuban?
Be that your task,
Go quickly as you can.

Your housewife's care forget;
The sun is nearly set.
Unlike the day
Stock-still *you* are;
Come, haste away,
Fetch the reluctant jar.

Green locks of Nereides,
And Neptune, Lord of Seas,
We celebrate,
And, to the lyre,
Latona great
And Cynthia's darts of fire.

To Her who Cnidos sees,
And shining Cyclades,
By yoke-swans white
Conveyed along—
To Her and Night
Shall rise our evensong.

George F. Whicher

Rustic Phidyle

Odes III, 23

Incense, and flesh of swine, and this year's grain,
  At the new moon, with suppliant hands, bestow,
O rustic Phidyle! So naught shall know
Thy crops of blight, thy vine of Afric bane,
And hale the nurslings of thy flock remain
Through the sick apple-tide. Fit victims grow
'Twixt holm and oak upon the Algid snow,
Or Alban grass, that with their necks must stain
The Pontiff's axe: to thee can scarce avail
Thy modest gods with much slain to assail,
Whom myrtle crowns and rosemary can please.
Lay on the altar a hand pure of fault;
More than rich gifts the Powers it shall appease,
Though pious but with meal and crackling salt.

Austin Dobson

The Anniversary

Odes III, 8

The first of March! and does it vex thy soul
    That I, a man unwed,
Have got me flowers and frankincense and coal
    On green grass-altar spread;

O skilled in lore of Greece and Italy?
    This he-goat white I vowed
As feast for Bacchus, when the falling tree
    Brought me so near my shroud.

So every year this day with cheery joke
    The rosin seals I'll strip
From jars laid up to mellow 'mid the smoke
    In Tullus' consulship.

Then take a hundred cups, Maecenas, for
    Thy friend's escape from harm;
Feed all the lamps till dawn: and bar the door
    To discord and alarm.

O'er weighty cares of State no longer brood;
    The Dacian Cottiso
And all his host are fallen; rent with feud
    Mede eyeth Mede as foe;

In Spain our enemies of long ago
    Are bound at last in chains;
At last the Scythian thinks to slack his bow
    And quit the conquered plains.

Then be an idle man, with ne'er a thought
    For how the people fare:
Content to take the gifts To-day has brought,
    And cry 'good-bye' to Care.

W. S. Marris

To Aristius Fuscus

Greetings from the Country

Epistles I, 10

Health, from the lover of the Country me,
    Health, to the lover of the City thee,
A difference in our souls, this only proves,
In all things else, w˘ agree like marryed doves.
But the warm nest, and crowded dove-house thou
Dost like; I loosly fly from bough to bough,
And Rivers drink, and all the shining day,
Upon fair Trees, or mossy Rocks I play;
In fine, I live and reign when I retire
From all that you equal with Heaven admire.
Like one at last from the Priests service fled,
Loathing the honie'd Cakes, I long for Bread.
Would I a house for happiness erect,
Nature alone should be the Architect.
She'd build it more convenient, then great,
And doubtless in the Country choose her seat.
Is there a place, doth better helps supply,
Against the wounds of Winters cruelty?
Is there an Ayr that gentl'er does asswage
The mad Celestial Dogs, or Lyons rage?
Is it not there that sleep (and only there)
Nor noise without, nor cares within does fear?
Does art through pipes, a purer water bring,
Then that which nature straines into a spring?
Can all your Tap'stries, or your Pictures show
More beauties then in herbs and flowers do grow?
Fountains and trees our wearied Pride do please,
Even in the midst of gilded Palaces.
And in your towns that prospect gives delight,
Which opens round the country to our sight.

Men to the good, from which they rashly fly,
Return at last, and their wild Luxury
Does but in vain with those true joyes contend,
Which Nature did to mankind recommend.
The man who changes gold for burnisht Brass,
Or small right Gems, for larger ones of glass:
Is not, at length, more certain to be made
Ridiculous, and wretched by the trade,
Than he, who sells a solid good, to buy
The painted goods of Pride and Vanity.
If thou be wise, no glorious fortune choose,
Which 'tis but pain to keep, yet grief to loose,
For, when we place even trifles, in the heart,
With trifles too, unwillingly we part.
An humble Room, plain bed, and homely board,
More clear, untainted pleasures do afford,
Then all the Tumult of vain greatness brings
To Kings, or to the favorites of Kings.
The horned Deer by Nature arm'd so well,
Did with the Horse in common pasture dwell;
And when they fought, the field it alwayes wan,
Till the ambitious Horse begg'd help of Man,
And took the bridle, and thenceforth did reign
Bravely alone, as Lord of all the plain:
But never after could the Rider get
From off his back, or from his mouth the bit.
So they, who poverty too much do fear,
T' avoid that weight, a greater burden bear;
That they might Pow'r above their equals have,
To cruel Masters they themselves enslave.
For Gold, their Liberty exchang'd we see,
That fairest flow'r, which crowns Humanity.
And all this mischief does upon them light,
Only, because they know not how, aright,
That great, but secret, happiness to prize,
That's laid up in a Little, for the Wise:
That is the best, and easiest Estate,
Which to a man sits close, but not too strait;

'Tis like a shooe; it pinches, and it burns,
Too narrow; and too large it overturns.
My dearest friend, stop thy desires at last,
And chearfully enjoy the wealth thou hast.
And, if me still seeking for more you see,
Chide, and reproach, despise and laugh at me.
Money was made, not to command our will,
But all our lawful pleasures to fulfil.
Shame and wo to us, if we our wealth obey;
The Horse doth with the Horse-man run away.

Abraham Cowley

Friends and Festivities

Since Horace was in the habit of addressing or dedicating each of his poems to a particular person, we know the names of many of his associates, friends, and patrons. But all too frequently little more than the name has come down to us. That is not the case, of course, with Virgil or Maecenas or Agrippa, names famous in the history of the Augustan Age. We know that Albius Tibullus was a writer of graceful poems of the type technically known, because of their verse form, as "elegies," that the scholarly Iccius was sometime procurator of Agrippa's estates in Sicily, and that Torquatus was a member of a family of well-to-do lawyers. Varius, Plotius, Quintilius are hardly less shadowy than Horace's Phyllis and Glycera. Of Pompeius, Aelius Lamia, and his comrade Numida, and many others nothing has been discovered beyond what Horace has told us. It is clear, however, that Horace was well known to a large circle of men of all sorts and conditions.

In the poet's scheme of values friendship occupied a prominent place. As he put it, "Nothing, while in my right mind, would I compare to the delight of a friend." He not only celebrated friendship in the abstract, but practiced it with diligent attention. We have numerous glimpses of Horace acting the part of host, but none more attractive than that disclosed in the ode addressed to a jar of Massic wine (III, 21) which is about to be opened in honor of a certain Corvinus, once a fellow student with Horace at Athens and like him a republican who had become reconciled to the empire. Another ode (IV, 12) shows him recommending the exchange of costly perfumes for wine to a certain Vergilius, surely less likely to be the poet Virgil than some one else of the same name. Again (Odes I, 27) he appears as the moderator at a drinking-bout that has threatened to become unruly, tactfully directing the conversation away from controversial topics and toward that theme of universal interest, womankind.

Of all Horace's friendships that with his patron Maecenas was most deeply felt. He could write jokingly to invite the urbane and wealthy statesman to share the homely delights and inexpensive vintages of his Sabine retreat (Odes I, 20). He could summon the lovely Phyllis to help him celebrate fittingly the birthday of his *alter ego* (Odes IV, 11). But the ode in which he links his own destiny with that of his friend (II, 17) was not lightly written. It was the expression of an entire dedication to the ideal of noble friendship, a devotion in which Horace found the fulfillment of the best side of his own loyal nature.

Bon Voyage for Virgil

Odes I, 3

So may th' auspicious Queen of Love,
And the Twin Stars (the Seed of *Jove*,)
And he who rules the rageing wind,
To thee, O sacred Ship, be kind;
And gentle Breezes fill thy sails,
Supplying soft *Etesian* Gales:
As thou, to whom the Muse commends
The best of Poets and of Friends,
Dost thy committed Pledge restore,
And land him safely on the shore;
And save the better part of me,
From perishing with him at Sea.
Sure he, who first the passage try'd,
In harden'd Oak his heart did hide,
And ribs of Iron arm'd his side;
Or his at least, in hollow wood
Who tempted first the briny Floud:
Nor fear'd the winds contending roar,
Nor billows beating on the Shoar;
Nor *Hyades* portending Rain;
Nor all the Tyrants of the Main.
What form of death cou'd him affright,
Who unconcern'd, with steadfast sight,
Cou'd veiw the Surges mounting steep,
And monsters rolling in the deep!
Cou'd thro' the ranks of ruin go,
With Storms above, and Rocks below!
In vain did Natures wise command
Divide the Waters from the Land,

If daring Ships, and Men prophane,
Invade th'inviolable Main;
Th' eternal Fences overleap,
And pass at will the boundless deep.
No toyl, no hardship can restrain
Ambitious Man, inur'd to pain;
The more confin'd, the more he tries,
And a forbidden quarry flies.
Thus bold *Prometheus* did aspire,
And stole from heav'n the seed of Fire:
A train of Ills, a ghastly crew,
The Robber's blazing track persue;
Fierce Famine, with her Meagre face,
And Feavours of the fiery Race,
In swarms th' offending Wretch surround
All brooding on the blasted ground:
And limping Death, lash'd on by Fate
Comes up to shorten half our date.
This made not *Dedalus* beware,
With borrow'd wings to sail in Air:
To Hell *Alcides* forc'd his way,
Plung'd thro' the Lake, and snatch'd the Prey.
Nay scarce the Gods, or heav'nly Climes,
Are safe from our audacious Crimes:
We reach at *Jove's* Imperial Crown,
And pull th' unwilling thunder down.

John Dryden

A Scholar Goes to War
Odes I, 29

Iccius, what change is here? You covet now
    Arabian treasures, and inflame your mind
Proud princes of Sabaea to o'erthrow
    And furious Medes to bind.

What Syrian damsel, widowed by your sword,
  From golden ewer shall bathe your conquering feet?
What curled and courtly page beside the board
  Shall serve you wine and meat,

Erst skilled to level from his father's bow
  Cathayan arrows? Who will now deny
That downward rivers up steep hills can flow,
  Or Tiber backward hie,

When you, from whom we hoped for better things,
  Swap the choice books you bought at every sale—
The best philosophers' best imaginings—
  For coats of Spanish mail?

Edward Marsh

Comrade in Arms

Odes II, 7

O, oft with me in troublous time
    Involved, when Brutus warred in Greece,
Who gives you back to your own clime
  And your own gods, a man of peace,
Pompey, the earliest friend I knew,
  With whom I oft cut short the hours
With wine, my hair bright bathed in dew
  Of Syrian oils, and wreathed with flowers?
With you I shared Philippi's rout,
  Unseemly parted from my shield,
When Valour fell, and warriors stout
  Were tumbled on the inglorious field:
But I was saved by Mercury,
  Wrapped in thick mist, yet trembling sore,
While you to that tempestuous sea
  Were swept by battle's tide once more.

Come, pay to Jove the feast you owe;
　　Lay down those limbs, with warfare spent,
Beneath my laurel; nor be slow
　　To drain my cask; for you 'twas meant.
Lethe's true draught is Massic wine;
　　Fill high the goblet; pour out free
Rich streams of unguent. Who will twine
　　The hasty wreath from myrtle-tree
Or parsley? Whom will Venus seat
　　Chairman of cups? Are Bacchants sane?
Then I'll be sober. O, 'tis sweet
　　To fool, when friends come home again.

John Conington

In Praise of Lamia

Odes I, 26

The Muse befriends me: gioom and care,
　　Be buried by the tempests' roar
In Cretic seas; beneath the Bear
　　What monarch rules the frozen shore,

Or wherefore Tiridates cowers,
　　I little reck. Pimplea sweet,
Nymph of pure springs, weave sunny flowers
　　For Lamia, weave him garlands neat.

I cannot waft his praise abroad
　　Without thee. Him with new-learned strain,
Him with the Lesbian quill to laud,
　　Befits thee and thy sister train.

Warren H. Cudworth

Numida Comes Home

Odes I, 36

Haste the tender victim bring;
   Strew the incense, strike the string!
Praise the gods, his guardian powers!
Numida again is ours.
Safe from Spain's remotest bound,
Lo! he greets his friends around,
Thee, my Lamia, o'er the rest
Clasping to his faithful breast;
Mindful that in childhood's play
Each obeyed one master's sway,
Mindful that, when manhood bloomed,
Each at once the robe assumed,
Let this day forever bright
Still be marked with Cretan white!
Let the cask's rich juice abound,
Beat with Salian dance the ground!
Nor shall Damalis surpass
Bassus in the cheerful glass.
Let gay flowers the board perfume,
Lillies breathe and roses bloom!
Damalis all eyes admire,
Eyes that gloat with fond desire,
Yet, as wanton ivy springs,
Faithful to her love she clings.

William Boscawen

A Feast for a Rainy Day

Odes III, 17

Aelius, thou of noble race,
　　From ancient Lamus who dost trace

Thine origin!—The tablets tell
The earlier Lamians as well

And all their proud descendants came
From such a source: thou hast thy name

From the great founder, who, men say,
Once held beneath his princely sway

The walls of Formiae and the stream
Of Liris, whose slow waters dream

There 'mid Marica's coasts,—at dawn
A tempest from the Orient drawn

Shall strew the groves with leaves, the shore
With useless seaweed cover o'er,

If long-lived crow that men believe
For augury do not deceive:

So while thou may, the faggots heap,
To-morrow thou a feast shalt keep;

With wine and sucking-pig shalt cheer
Thy guardian spirit and endear

Thyself to all the slaves while they
Share the unlooked-for holiday.

A. L. Taylor

To a Jar of Wine
Odes III, 21

O precious crock, whose summers date,
   Like mine, from Manlius' consulate,
I wot not whether in your breast
Lie maudlin wail or merry jest,
Or sudden choler, or the fire
Of tipsy Love's insane desire,
Or fumes of soft caressing sleep,
Or what more potent charms you keep,
But this I know, your ripened power
Befits some choicely festive hour!
A cup peculiarly mellow
Corvinus asks; so come, old fellow,
From your time-honoured bin descend,
And let me gratify my friend!
No churl is he, your charms to slight,
Though most intensely erudite:
And even old Cato's worth, we know,
Took from good wine a nobler glow.

Your magic power of wit can spread
The halo round a dullard's head,
Can make the sage forget his care,
His bosom's inmost thoughts unbare,
And drown his solemn-faced pretence
Beneath your blithesome influence.
Bright hope you bring and vigour back
To minds outworn upon the rack,
And put such courage in the brain,
As makes the poor be men again,
Whom neither tyrants' wrath affrights,
Nor all their bristling satellites.

Bacchus, and Venus, so that she
Bring only frank festivity,

With sister Graces in her train,
Twining close in lovely chain,
And gladsome tapers' living light,
Shall spread your treasures o'er the night,
Till Phoebus the red East unbars,
And puts to rout the trembling stars.

Sir Theodore Martin

Invitation to Maecenas

Odes I, 20

Since thou, Maecenas, nothing loth,
    Under the bard's roof-tree,
Canst drink rough wine of Sabine growth,
    Here stands a jar for thee!—
    The Grecian delf I sealed myself,
        That year the theatre broke forth
        In tribute to thy sterling worth.

When Rome's glad shout the welkin rent,
    Along the Tiber ran,
And rose again, by Echo sent,
    Back from Mount Vatican;—
    When with delight, O Roman knight!
        Etruria heard her oldest flood
        Do homage to her noblest blood.

Wines of Falernian vintage, friend,
    Thy princely cellar stock;
Bethink thee, should'st thou condescend
    To share a poet's crock,
    Its modest shape, Cajeta's grape
        Hath never tinged, nor Formia's hill
        Deigned with a purple flood to fill.

Francis Sylvester Mahony

Love's the Alibi

Epode 14

You ask, what means this torpid indolence
   That in oblivion every sense
Has steep'd, as if my thirsty lips had quaff'd
   At Lethe's spring a copious draught?—
And kill me by remonstrance without end:
   A God—a God denies, my friend!
All power the promised stanzas to compose,
   And bring my fragment to a close;
Love, mighty Love the vein of song has marr'd!
   So glow'd of old the Teian bard—
So in wild measures to the plaintive shell
   Mourn'd the coy jilt he loved so well.
Yourself, no stranger to the pleasing pain,
   Are caught, like me, in Cupid's chain.
But, if a fairer flame beleaguer'd not
   Troy's towers, commend your happy lot!
My thoughts on humble Phryne now are bent,
   A freed-girl—nor with *one* content.

Francis Howes

Not to Be Parted

Odes II, 17

No! My Maecenas, no! the gods and I
   Are clearly averse, that thou shouldst die;
My best support, my patron, or to blend
Every dear name in one, my honoured friend,
Cease these complaints, it cannot, must not be,
That thou shouldst seek Elysium without me.

Alas! should fate the hasty mandate give,
And my soul's better part should cease to live;
Then for what reason should I tarry here,
Not half so good, nor to mankind so dear;
Nor could I long survive, when torn from thee;
The day, which takes thee hence, will ruin me.

Have I not sworn, nor will I break my oath,
The call of death for one will summon both;
When, or howe'er thou may'st the journey make,
I am resolv'd its perils to partake;
We will together, tread the gloomy way,
Together, seek the realms of brighter day.

Though to appal me, fell Chimera stands,
Though Gyas rise, and with his hundred hands
Oppose my passage, nought shall have the pow'r,
To tear me from thee in that dreadful hour;
In life, in death, resolv'd to follow thee,
Justice demands it, and the fates decree.

For whether Libra, balance of the earth,
Or the fierce scorpion overruled our birth,
Or the rude tyrant of the western sea;
Certain, our stars most strangely do agree;
Jupiter's guardian glories round thee shine,
While light-wing'd Mercury's protection's mine.

For when cold Saturn would repress thy praise,
Thy planet rules, and lo! the people raise
Three shouts of glad applause; and when on me
The fatal sisters hurl'd a falling tree,
Mercury, watchful patron of the learn'd,
Aside by Faunus' hand the danger turn'd.

Remember therefore, to the Gods to fête,
Victims to burn, and temples dedicate;
For thee, the smoke of hecatombs shall rise,
But for thy Horace one poor lamb suffice.

Susanna Rowson

Maecenas' Birthday

Odes IV, 11

Here, Phyllis, is a cask of Alban juice
  O'er nine years mellowed: here my garth supplies,
For twining chaplets, parsley leaves profuse;
  Here ivies lushly rise

Which, twisted in thy locks, become thee so;
  My house with silver gleams; the altar, hung
With holy vervain, longs for blood to flow
  From votive lambkin young.

The household all is busy; here and there
  Maids grouped with pages haste their help to lend;
And, swirling from the bickering hearth-fire's glare,
  The sooty fumes ascend.

Yet wouldst thou know what joys invite thee here?
  We celebrate the Ides, whose day in twain
Cuts April, month to Venus ever dear,
  The daughter of the main.

'Tis rightly festal and I scarcely deem
  My own birthday more blest, since from this day
My friend Maecenas counts his years that stream
  In lapsing flight away.

For Telephus, whose rank o'ertops thine own,
  Thou pinest; but a girl, a rich coquette,
Allured him, and her pleasing fetters, thrown
  About him, hold him yet.

Scorched Phaethon from vaunting aims should fright,
  And Pegasus taught lesson grave anew,
When, irked by earth-born rider in his flight,
  Bellerophon he threw,

Ever to seek what fits thee and allow,
  Since hopes beyond thy sphere conduce to shame,
No thought of ill-matched nuptials. Therefore, now,
  Come, last and dearest flame

(For ne'er another woman shall consume
  My heart), and learn my cadences; erelong
Thy lovely voice shall lilt them: cares and gloom
  Flee the approach of song.

                                   Warren H. Cudworth

To Ligurinus

Odes IV, 10

Though mighty in Love's favor still,
    Though cruel yet, my boy,
When the unwelcome dawn shall chill
    Your pride and youthful joy,
The hair which round your shoulder grows
    Is rudely cut away,
Your color, redder than the rose,
    Is changed by youth's decay,—

Then, Ligurinus, in the glass
    Another you will spy.
And as the shaggy face, alas!
    You see, your grief will cry:
"Why in my youth could I not learn
    The wisdom men enjoy?
Or why to men cannot return
    The smooth cheeks of the boy?"

                                   Roswell Martin Field

To Vergilius
Odes IV, 12

Now blow the Thracian breezes, Spring's companions,
That soothe the seas and waft the vessels onward;
No longer meads are frost-bound, nor the rivers
    Roar with the swelling from wintry snow-drifts.

Now nests the luckless bird, lamenting sorely
Her Itys—she, of the old house of Cecrops
Eternal shame! for there she wrought foul vengeance
    Barbarous lust of the kings requiting.

Now in the tender grass the flocks are feeding,
Their guardian shepherds piping songs of springtime
To joy the god to whom the flocks are pleasing,
    Lover of dusky Arcadian ridges.

The thirsty hours have come apace, my Vergil;
If thou wouldst quaff the juice trod out at Cales,
Then buy the wine, O client of young nobles!
    Paying rich price of Orient perfume.

An onyx vase of nard will lure a wine-jar
Now slumbering in the storehouse of Sulpitius,
Endued with power to build thy hopes more largely,
    Driving away all thy bitter sorrows.

If joys like these thou art in haste to welcome,
Come swiftly with thy merchandise. I plan not
That thou shouldst bring no share, yet drain my goblets,
    Deeming me rich and housed in fulness.

So cast aside delay and zeal for riches
Remembering how death's gloomy fires await us.
And while thou mayst, mix folly with thy wisdom.
    Sweet is it sometimes to play the witling.

George Meason Whicher

A Proper Feast

Odes I, 27

Come, comrades, cease your Thracian fights
   O'er cups designed for better uses,
For moderate Bacchus ne'er delights
   In bloody quarrels o'er his juices.

How far removed from lamps and wine
   Should be the Median dagger keen!
Hush drunken clamor, friends of mine;
   In quiet on your elbows lean.

. . . You wish to have me taste my share
   Of strong Falernian with the rest?—
Megilla's brother must declare
   First, by what mortal wound he's blest.

Falters his will?—Then I'll not drink—
   Come, tell us by what love you're swayed,
What fire consumed;—tut, man, don't shrink
   To own an honest escapade!

Trust it to safe ears; 'tis no sin
   But to impart your sweetheart's name . . .
Ah! what Charybdis are you in,
   Youth worthy of a nobler flame!

What witch, what wizard's potent brew,
   What god can save you this time, sirrah?
Scarce Pegasus could rescue you,
   Entrapped by such three-fold Chimera.

George F. Whicher

A Stormy Night for Revelry

Epode 13

With storm and wrack the sky is black, and sleet and dashing
      rain
With all the gathered streams of heaven are deluging the plain;
Now roars the sea, the forests roar with the shrill north wind of
      Thrace,
Then let us snatch the hour, my friends, the hour that flies apace,
Whilst yet the bloom is on our cheeks, and rightfully we may
With song and jest and jollity keep wrinkled age at bay!
Bring forth a jar of lordly wine, whose years my own can mate,
Its ruby juices stained the vats in Torquatus' consulate!
No word of anything that's sad; whate'er may be amiss
The Gods belike will change to some vicissitude of bliss!
With Achaemenian nard bedew our locks, and troubles dire
Subdue to rest in every breast with the Cyllenian lyre!
So to his peerless pupil once the noble Centaur sang:
"Invincible, yet mortal, who from goddess Thetis sprang,
Thee waits Assaracus's realm, where arrowy Simois glides,
That realm which chill Scamander's rill with scanty stream divides,
Whence never more shalt thou return,—the Parcae so decree,
Nor shall thy blue-eyed mother home again e'er carry thee.
Then chase with wine and song divine each grief and trouble there,
The sweetest, surest antidotes of beauty-marring care!"

                        Sir Theodore Martin

To Albius Tibullus
The Maxims of a Jovial Epicurean
Epistles I, 4

Albius, in whom my satires find
    A candid critic, and a kind,
Do you, while at your country seat,
Some rhyming labours meditate,
That shall in volumed bulk arise,
And even from Cassius bear the prize;
Or saunter through the silent wood,
Musing on what befits the wise and good?
  Thou art not form'd of lifeless mould,
With breast inanimate and cold;
To thee the gods a form complete,
To thee the gods a fair estate
In bounty gave, with art to know
How to enjoy what they bestow.
  Can a fond nurse one blessing more
Even for her favourite boy implore,
With sense and clear expression bless'd,
Of friendship, honour, health possess'd,
A table, elegantly plain,
And a poetic, easy vein?
  By hope inspired, depress'd with fear,
By passion warm'd, perplex'd with care,
Believe, that every morning's ray
Hath lighted up the latest day;
Then, if tomorrow's sun be thine,
With double lustre shall it shine.
  Such are the maxims I embrace,
And here, in sleek and joyous case,
You'll find, for laughter fitly bred,
A hog by Epicurus fed.

Philip Francis

To Torquatus

An Invitation to Dine

Epistles I, 5

If you can lie, Torquatus, when you take
    Your meal, upon a couch of Archias' make,
And sup off potherbs, gathered as they come,
You'll join me, please, by sunset at my home.
My wine, not far from Sinuessa grown,
Is but six years in bottle, I must own:
If you've a better vintage, send it here,
Or take your cue from him who finds the cheer.
My hearth is swept, my household looks its best,
And all my furniture expects a guest.
Forego your dreams of riches and applause,
Forget e'en Moschus' memorable cause;
To-morrow's Caesar's birthday, which we keep
By taking, to begin with, extra sleep;
So, if with pleasant converse we prolong
This summer night, we scarcely shall do wrong.
    Why should the Gods have put me at my ease,
If I mayn't use my fortune as I please?
The man who stints and pinches for his heir
Is next-door neighbour to a fool, I'll swear.
Here, give me flowers to strew, my goblet fill,
And let men call me mad-cap if they will.
O, drink is mighty! secrets it unlocks,
Turns hope to fact, sets cowards on to box,
Takes burdens from the careworn, finds out parts
In stupid folks, and teaches unknown arts.
What tongue hangs fire when quickened by the bowl?
What wretch so poor but wine expands his soul?
    Meanwhile, I'm bound in duty, nothing loth,
To see that nought in coverlet or cloth

May give you cause to sniff, that dish and cup
May serve you as a mirror while you sup;
To have my guests well-sorted, and take care
That none is present who'll tell tales elsewhere.
You'll find friend Butra and Septicius here,
Ditto Sabinus, failing better cheer:
And each might bring a friend or two as well,
But then, you know, close packing's apt to smell.
Come, name your number, and elude the guard
Your client keeps by slipping through the yard.

John Conington

Pretty Ladies

This section may appropriately begin with a formal invocation to Venus and end with two poems addressed to the same goddess wherein the poet protests that his days of love-making are over. And when, we may inquire, was the time of sweet dalliance that he referred to as "the reign of the good Cinara"? If Horace ever had a mistress of that name, he wrote no poems in her honor. None of his lyrics are inspired by the passion of a Catullus or a Robert Burns. They were the cool comments of an onlooker, amused by the game of sentiment. If Horace was indeed the old hand at courtship that he claimed to be, he took good care not to write until his emotions could be safely recollected in tranquillity.

Not improbably some of the daintiest of his poems on feminine allure and evasiveness, such as the famous odes To Pyrrha (I, 5) and To Chloe (I, 23), were closely imitated from Greek originals and represent an exercise in delicate versification rather than in amorous excitation on the poet's part. No Greek, however, would have written the *Integer Vitae* (I, 22), which is so clearly two poems in one that it could be translated by John Quincy Adams as a compliment to a lady and by Thomas Campion as a eulogy of the upright man, with no "love interest" whatever. The ode called The Satirist's Recantation (I, 16) is often supposed to be an apology on Horace's part to some charmer who had been offended by his verses. But very few of the pieces dealing with love of woman have even that much basis in actuality.

Since no part of Horace's writing has been better liked, for the last four hundred years at least, than these poems on women and their ways, it may be plausibly argued that a poet writes best when his substance is drawn largely from his imagination and his whole attention is centered on the problem of expression. Horace's dainty mistresses, like Robert Herrick's, would appear to owe their existence mainly to the faculty of invention.

> *All were but syllabled air,*
> *Fancies that flickered and flew:*
> *Innocent Phidyle's prayer,*
> *Chloe the fawn, and the few*
> *Years that your Cinara knew,*
> *Cinara, sweetest of flames!*
> *Ah! Horace, I'm sorry for you!*
> *Alas! they were nothing but names.*

Calling Venus

Odes I, 30

Come, Cnidian, Paphian Venus, come,
  Thy well-beloved Cyprus spurn,
Haste, where for thee in Glycera's home
  Sweet odours burn.
Bring too thy Cupid, glowing warm,
  Graces and Nymphs, unzoned and free,
And Youth, that lacking thee lacks charm,
  And Mercury.

John Conington

Love Mocks Us All

Odes I, 33

Love mocks us all. Then cast aside
  These tuneful plaints, my Albius tried
  For heartless Glycera, from thee
  Fled to a younger lover. See,
Low-browed Lycoris burns denied

For Cyrus; he—though goats shall bide
With wolves ere she in him confide—
  Turns, with base suit, to Pholoe:—
    Love mocks us all!

So Venus wills, and joys to guide
'Neath brazen yoke pairs ill-allied
  In form and mind. So linked she me
  (Whom worthier wooed) to Myrtale,
Fair, but less kind than Hadria's tide:—
  Love mocks us all!

Austin Dobson

An Old Flame Rekindled

Odes I, 19

The tyrant queen of soft desires,
  With the resistless aid of sprightly wine
  And wanton ease, conspires
To make my heart its peace resign,
And re-admit love's long-rejected fires.
  For beauteous Glycera I burn,
The flames so long repell'd with double force return.
Matchless her face appears, and shines more bright
Than polish'd marble when reflecting light:
    Her very coyness warms;
  And with a grateful sullenness she charms:
  Each look darts forth a thousand rays,
  Whose lustre an unwary sight betrays;
My eye-balls swim, and I grow giddy while I gaze.

  She comes! she comes! she rushes in my veins!
At once all Venus enters, and at large she reigns!
  Cyprus no more with her abode is blest,
  I am her palace, and her throne my breast.
  Of savage Scythian arms no more I write,
  Of Parthian archers, who in flying fight,
    And make rough war their sport;
  Such idle themes no more can move,

Nor anything but what's of high import:
And what's of high import, but love?
Vervain and gums, and the green turf prepare;
With wine of two years old your cups be fill'd:
After our sacrifice and prayer,
The goddess may incline her heart to yield.

William Congreve

The Traitress

Epode 15

Night—and in a windless sky rode the radiant moon on high
In the midst of her attendant starry train,
When to me you plighted troth, repeating after me the oath—
Yet you meant to take the Gods' names in vain!
And as oak is by ivy enclasped, lost love,
Your arms clung close; and you swore,
"I'll be true, long as sheep fear the wolf; long as leap
The billows when winter winds roar;

Long as summer breeze caresses Apollo's flowing tresses,
I'll be true, will render love for love to thee!"
O Neaera, you shall rue it! By my manly soul, I'll do it!—
Or else there's not a spark of man in me!
I will see not a rival have all, lost love,
That was mine. There are fairer and truer:
And the heart that has loved you, and traitress proved you,
Stoops not to your beauty's lure.

And you, my favored rival crowing now, "I'm the survival
Of the fittest!"—since I'm left out in the cold;—
Though your flocks be past the telling, and your rent-roll ever swell-
ing,

Though everything you touch turn to gold;
  Be you wise with the wisdom of old, poor fool,
    Be you fair as the fairest of men,—
Ha! you yet shall have reason to weep for her treason
  While I laugh—'Twill be my turn then!

Arthur S. Way

To Pyrrha

Odes I, 5

What slender Youth, bedew'd with liquid odours,
    Courts thee on Roses in some pleasant Cave,
Pyrrha? For whom bindst thou
  In wreaths thy golden Hair,
Plain in thy neatness? O how oft shall he
On Faith and changéd Gods complain, and seas
  Rough with black winds, and storms
  Unwonted shall admire!
Who now enjoyes thee credulous, all Gold,
Who always vacant, always amiable
  Hopes thee, of flattering gales
  Unmindfull. Hapless they
To whom thou untry'd seem'st fair. Me in my vow'd
Picture the sacred wall declares t'have hung
  My dank and dropping weeds
  To the stern God of Sea.

John Milton

One More Unfortunate

Odes I, 5

What Stripling now Thee discomposes,
    In Woodbine Rooms, on Beds of Roses,
For whom thy Auburn Haire
Is spread, Unpainted Faire?
How will he one day curse thy Oaths
And Heav'n that witness'd your Betroaths!
    How will the poor Cuckold,
    That deems thee perfect Gold,
Bearing no stamp but his, be mas'd
To see a suddain Tempest rais'd!
    He dreams not of the Windes,
    And thinks all Gold that shines.
For me my Votive Table showes
That I have hung up my wet Clothes
    Upon the Temple Wall
    Of Seas great Admirall.

Sir Richard Fanshawe

Speaking from Experience

Odes I, 5

What perfumed, posie-dizened sirrah,
    With smiles for diet,
Clasps you, O fair but faithless Pyrrha,
    On the quiet?
For whom do you bind up your tresses,
    As spun-gold yellow,—
Meshes that go with your caresses,
    To snare a fellow?

How will he rail at fate capricious,
   And curse you duly,
Yet now he deems your wiles delicious,—
   You perfect, truly!
Pyrrha, your love's a treacherous ocean;
   He'll soon fall in there!
Then shall I gloat on his commotion,
   For *I* have been there!

                      Eugene Field

A Tale to Touch the Heart

Odes III, 11

O! Mercury, whose master-tones
   Amphion learnt and moved the stones,
And, tortoise-shell, whose music rings
   From seven strings,

Once neither sweet nor musical
But welcome now to shrine and hall,
Teach me a song to hold at last
   Coy Lyde fast,

Who, as a filly, three years old
That, shy and skittish, roams the wold,
Is all unripe for wedlock's bliss,
   And shuns a kiss.

You stay the running streams: on you
Tigers attend and forests too:
The vasty forecourt's guard was ta'en
   By your sweet strain,

Cerberus, whose head the Furies' wreath
Guards with the hundred snakes: his breath
Is noisome: from his triple lips
   Blood reeks and drips.

Ixion ev'n perforce, must smile,
Ev'n Tityos: that urn, the while
The girls of Danaus you thrilled,
   Was left unfilled.

Let Lyde hear the maidens' sin
And doom, the water running in
And out: the empty cask; tho' late,
   The hand of Fate

Laid on the guilty, here or there.
Unnatural! even this to dare!
Unnatural, who the self-same day
   Could wed and slay!

But one to her false father lied,
One out of many, worthy bride
Alone,—the glory of that lie
   Can never die—

Who to her bridegroom cried, "Begone:
Lest the long sleep be yours from one
You guess not: your new father, my
   False sisters fly.

Ev'n now, as lionesses kine,
Each rends her mate: this heart of mine
Is gentle; cannot slay you, dear,
   Or chain you here.

Bonds or whate'er my father will,
Because my love I would not kill,
For me: for me, an exile banned,
   The Afric sand.

But you, while night and Venus aid,
By land and sea go unafraid:
God guard you: on my grave record
   One loving word."

Hugh MacNaghten

Precedents for Xanthias
Odes II, 4

Blush not, my Friend, to own the Love
    Which thy fair Captive's Eyes do move:
Achilles, once, the Fierce, the Brave,
    Stoopt to the Beauties of a Slave;
Tecmessa's charms could overpower
    Ajax her lord and Conquerour.
Great Agamemnon, when success
    Did all his Arms with Conquest bless;
When Hector's fall had gained him more
    Than ten long rolling Years before,
By a bright Captive Virgin's Eyes,
    Even in the midst of Triumph dies.
You know not to what mighty line
    The lovely Maid may make you join;
See but the Charms her Sorrow wears,
    No common Cause could draw such Tears:
Those Streams sure that adorn her so
    For Loss of Royal Kindred flow:
Oh! think not so divine a thing
    Could from the Bed of Commons spring;
Whose Faith could so unmov'd remain,
    And so averse to sordid Gain,
Was never born of any Race
    That might the noblest Love disgrace.
Her blooming Face, her snowy Arms,
    Her well shap'd Leg and all the Charms
Of her Body and her Face,
    I, poor I, may safely praise.
Suspect not Love, the youthful Rage,
    From Horace's declining Age.
But think removed by forty Years,
    All his Flames and all thy Fears.

Richard Duke

To Lydia

Odes I, 13

When you to Telephus devote,
  O Lydia, your choicest phrases,
And either Telephus' white throat
  Or wax-like arms excite your praises,
Bah! my disgusted anger surges
Like waves which stormy Notus urges.

Then I am blinded by my wrath,
  And quite unstable my complexion;
While on my cheek a tear-stained path
  Shows how I mourn your changed affection.
For when to me you're ever lost
I burn, a lingering holocaust.

I burn to think how, mad with wine,
  That boy in drunken rage may mar
With blows those gleaming arms of thine,
  Or leave upon thy lips a scar.
Ah! who could that fair mouth abuse
Which Venus with all sweets endues!

O thrice and four times blessèd they
  Whose life no evil quarrel knows,
But calm and peaceful day by day
  Glides as a quiet river flows;
Whom an unbroken bond holds ever
Until the last sad day shall sever.

George F. Whicher

Like a Fawn

Odes I, 23

Why, whenever she can spy me,
  Like a fawn will Chloe fly me?
Like a fawn, its mother seeking
O'er the hills, through brambles breaking;
Frightened if the breezes move
But a leaflet in the grove;
Or a branch the Zephyr tosses;
Or its path a Lizard crosses;
Nothing can its fear dissemble—
Heart and knees together tremble.
  Stop, my love; Thou needst not fear me.
For I follow not to tear thee
Like the Lion, prowling o'er
Far Letulia's savage shore:
Stop—Thy budding charms discover
'Tis thy time to choose a lover.

Patrick Branwell Brontë

To Chloe

Odes I, 23

You shun me, Chloe, wild and shy,
  As some stray fawn that seeks its mother
Through trackless woods. If spring winds sigh
  It vainly strives its fears to smother.
Its trembling knees assail each other
  When lizards stir the brambles dry;—
You shun me, Chloe, wild and shy,
  As some stray fawn that seeks its mother.

And yet no Libyan lion I,—
　No ravening thing to rend another;
Lay by your tears, your tremors dry,
　A husband's better than a brother;
Nor shun me, Chloe, wild and shy,
　As some stray fawn that secks its mother.

Austin Dobson

Too Young

Odes II, 5

Y our heifer's pretty neck is not yet broke
　To stand the pressure of a husband's yoke;
She's too young yet to bear the weight
And duties of the marriage state.
Round the green meadows with the steers to stray
She loves, or in moist osier-beds to play,
　Or her sun-heated flanks to lave
　In some cool brook's refreshing wave.
Let not blind passion make you over bold:
Your grasp from yonder unripe grapes withhold,
　That Autumn soon with purple hue
　Of varied tint will paint for you.
The wings of Time beat fast, and every year
He takes away from you, he adds to her:
　With flashing eye and flushing cheek
　Soon Lalage your love will seek.
Not Chloris then with her developed charms
Will vie, nor Pholoe, who flies your arms,
　Her shoulders beautiful and bright
　As moonbeams on the sea at night.
Not Gyges' self will then with her compare;
Though, 'midst a troop of girls, his flowing hair
　And fair smooth face might well perplex
　A stranger to discern his sex.

Thomas Charles Baring

"Tears, Idle Tears . . ."

Odes III, 7

Why are you weeping for Gyges?
    Your lover, though absent, is true.
As soon as warm weather obliges,
    He'll come back to you.

At Oricus, snow-bound and grieving,
    He yearns for domestic delights.
He longs for the moment of leaving;
    He lies awake nights.

His hostess, a lady of fashion,
    Is trying to fan up a few
Stray flames of his fiery passion,
    Lit only for you.

With sighs and suggestive romances
    She does what a sorceress can.
But Gyges—he scorns her advances;
    The noble young man.

But you—how about your bold neighbor?
    Does he please your still lachrymose eye?
When he gallops past, flashing his saber,
    Do you watch him go by?

When he swims, like a god, down the river,
    Do you dry the perpetual tear?
Does your heart give the least, little quiver?
    Be careful, my dear.

Be warned, and be deaf to his pleadings;
    To all of his questions be mute.
Do not heed any soft intercedings
    That rise from his flute.

Lock up when the day has departed,
   Though the music grows plaintive or shrill.
And though he may call you hard-hearted,
   Be obdurate still!

Louis Untermeyer

The Roman Debutante

Odes III, 12

It would seem a girl is doomed to be a saint:
   They tell us what we may and what we mayn't!
     We mustn't have affairs,
     We mustn't drown our cares,
Or we're lectured by an uncle till we faint.

Any morning, if I start to spin my wool,
Or do the useful things I learnt at school,
     Comes Cupid on the wing
     To set me wondering
Where Hebrus is, and then my thoughts are full.

Is he riding like a new Bellerophon,
Or swimming up the Tiber in the sun
     With his body shining white?
     Is he finishing a fight,
Or passing all the champions in a run?

Is he shooting at the stags that wildly fly
Across the plains in maddened company,
     Or when the great boar rushes
     From his covert in the bushes,
Is he ready with his dart to pierce its eye?

Edward Marsh

Integer Vitae

Odes I, 22

He who is innocent and pure
   Needs not to go equipped
With spear or quiver of the Moor
   And arrows poison-tipped.

Not though he fare through Syrtes' waves,
   Cold Caucasus' expanse,
Or regions that Hydaspes laves,
   That river of romance.

I roamed beyond my farm at ease,
   I sang of Lalage,
And met unarmed among the trees
   A wolf, who fled from me.

Martial Apulia, forest-land,
   Bred never monster worse;
Nor such was weaned 'mid Juba's sand
   The lions' thirsty nurse.

Set me on steppes, where summer air
   No leaf hath ever kissed,
The zone that lies in dull despair
   Of sombre sky and mist;

Set me where flames so fierce a heat
   That there no dwellers be:
Yet will I love her—smiling-sweet,
   Sweet-speaking Lalage.

W. S. Marris

To Sally

Odes I, 22

The man in righteousness arrayed,
   A pure and blameless liver,
Needs not the keen Toledo blade,
   Nor venom-freighted quiver.
What though he wind his toilsome way
   O'er regions wild and weary—
Through Zara's burning desert stray,
   Or Asia's jungles dreary:

What though he plow the billowy deep
   By lunar light, or solar,
Meet the resistless Simoom's sweep,
   Or iceberg circumpolar!
In bog or quagmire deep and dank
   His foot shall never settle;
He mounts the summit of Mont Blanc,
   Or Popocatapetl.

On Chimborazo's breathless height
   He treads o'er burning lava;
Or snuffs the Bohan Upas blight,
   The deathful plant of Java.
Through every peril he shall pass,
   By Virtue's shield protected;
And still by Truth's unerring glass
   His path shall be directed.

Else wherefore was it, Thursday last,
   While strolling down the valley,
Defenseless, musing as I passed
   A canzonet to Sally,

A wolf, with mouth-protruding snout,
　　Forth from the thicket bounded—
I clapped my hands and raised a shout—
　　He heard—and fled—confounded.

Tangier nor Tunis never bred
　　An animal more crabbéd;
Nor Fez, dry-nurse of lions, fed
　　A monster half so rabid;
Nor Ararat so fierce a beast
　　Has seen since days of Noah;
Nor stronger, eager for a feast,
　　The fell constrictor boa.

Oh! place me where the solar beam
　　Has scorch'd all verdure vernal;
Or on the polar verge extreme,
　　Block'd up with ice eternal—
Still shall my voice's tender lays
　　Of love remain unbroken;
And still my charming Sally praise,
　　Sweet smiling and sweet spoken.

John Quincy Adams

Impatient

Odes III, 10

Before thy doors too long of late,
　　O Lyce, I bewail my fate;
Not Don's barbarian maids, I trow,
　　Would treat their luckless lovers so;
Thou,—thou alone art obstinate.

Hast thou nor eyes nor ears, Ingrate!
Hark! how the NORTH WIND shakes thy gate!
   Look! how the laurels bend with snow
     Before thy doors!

Lay by thy pride, nor hesitate,
Lest Love and I grow desperate;
   If prayers, if gifts for naught must go,
   If naught my frozen pallor show,—
Beware! . . . I shall not always wait
     Before thy doors!

               Austin Dobson

Why Indeed?

Odes I, 8

Lydia, in Heavens Name
   Why melts yong Sybaris in thy Flame?
Why doth he bed-rid lie
   That can indure th' intemp'rate Skie?
Why rides he not and twits
   The French great Horse with wringled bits?
Why shuns he Tybur's Flood,
   And wrastlers Oyle like Vipers Blood?
Nor hath His Flesh made soft
   With bruising Arms; having so oft
Been prais'd for shooting farre
   And clean delivered of the Barre?
For shame, why lies he hid
   As at Troy's Siege Achilles did,
For fear lest Mans Array
   Should Him to Manly Deeds betray?

           Sir Richard Fanshawe

Getting Lydia's Number

Odes I, 8

Lydia, by the gods above,
    Tell me why, O maid magnetic,
You must ruin with your love
    Him that used to be athletic?

Tell me why, O maid magnetic,
    Sybaris will not cavort—
Him that used to be athletic,
    Him that used to be a sport?

Sybaris will not cavort
    On the field or in the river—
Him that used to be a sport
    With the quoit or with the quiver!

On the field or in the river,
    On the court or on the links,
With the quoit or with the quiver—
    You're his Jonah, you're his Jinx!

On the court or on the links
    Sybaris was once a wonder,
You're his Jonah, you're his Jinx—
    Why delight to drag him under?

Sybaris was once a wonder
    You must ruin with your love.
Why delight to drag him under?
    Lydia, by the gods above!

Franklin P. Adams

Baleful Barine

Odes II, 8

Barine, had there aught of harm
Befallen thee from broken vow,—
Hadst thou but lost a single charm,
Less fair become in eye or brow,—
    I might believe thee now.

But thou, as soon as thou dost stake
Thy head with some perfidious prayer,
More lovely yet thy form dost make,
To all the youth a toast more rare,
    Thy fatal face more fair!

Yea, by thy buried mother's shade
It only profits thee to lie;
And thou hast flouted, unafraid,
The speechless stars in all the sky,
    And gods that never die.

And Venus' self at this has laughed;
The simple Nymphs will laugh, I say;
And Cupid, too, whose fiery shaft
On his blood-dripping stone alway
    He whets day after day.

Add one count more: there ever grow
Still other youths, all slaves for thee!
While yet no earlier victims go,—
None from their impious mistress flee,
    Whate'er their threatnings be!

All mothers dread thee for their boys;
And old men fear thee, misers grown;
And piteous brides, on whose new joys
But once thy deadly breath has blown,
    To make them all thine own.

George Meason Whicher

"The Female of the Species"
Odes III, 20

Have you ever robbed a lioness of just one tiny whelp?
  Have you ever felt the power of her claws?
Well, think of these, oh Pyrrhus, and before you cry for help,
Remember what a woman is—and pause.

The unfair sex, the one that is "more deadly than the male,"
  Will never leave unturned a single stone,
She'll fight, she'll bite, she'll scorn the rules; she'll make a strong
    man pale . . .
So you'd better let Nearchus quite alone.

And meanwhile this Nearchus, the sweet and blushing prize,
  Conducts himself as umpire of the fray;
He shakes his scented locks; he smirks and rolls his pretty eyes—
  A tired semi-demi-god at play.

Oh let her have her perfumed youth—as she is sure to do,
  Although she break a Senate-full of laws;
Admit defeat. Retreat from them—the virgin or the shrew.
  Remember what a woman is—and pause.

Louis Untermeyer

The Satirist's Recantation
Odes I, 16

Blest with a charming mother, yet
    Thou still more fascinating daughter!
Prythee my vile lampoons forget—
Give to the flames the libel—let
    The satire sink in Adria's water!

Not Cybele's most solemn rites,
  Cymbals of brass and spells of magic;
Apollo's priest, 'mid Delphic flights;
Or Bacchanal, 'mid fierce delights,
  Presents a scene more tragic

Than Anger, when it rules the soul.
  Nor fire nor sword can then surmount her,
Nor the vex'd elements control,
Though Jove himself, from pole to pole,
  Thundering rush down to the encounter.

Prometheus—forced to graft, of old,
  Upon our stock a foreign scion,
Mix'd up—if we be truly told—
With some brute particles, our mould—
  Anger he gathered from the lion.

Anger destroyed Thyestes' race,
  O'erwhelmed his house in ruin thorough,
And many a lofty city's trace
Caused a proud foeman to efface,
  Ploughing the site with hostile furrow.

Oh, be appeased! 'twas rage, in sooth,
  First woke my song's satiric tenor;
In wild and unreflecting youth,
Anger inspired the deed uncouth;
  But, pardon that foul misdemeanour.

Lady! I swear—my recreant lays
  Henceforth to rectify and alter—
To change my tones from blame to praise,
Should your rekindling friendship raise
  The spirits of a sad defaulter!

                Francis Sylvester Mahony

Invitation to Tyndaris
Odes I, 17

Oft for the hill where ranges
     My Sabine flock,
Swift-footed Faun exchanges
     Arcadia's rock,
And, tempering summer's ray, forbids
Untoward rain to harm my kids.

And there in happy vagrance,
     Roams the she-goat,
Lured by marital fragrance,
     Through dells remote;
Of each wild herb and shrub partakes,
Nor fears the coil of lurking snakes.

No prowling wolves alarm her;
     Safe from their gripe
While Faun, immortal charmer!
     Attunes his pipe,
And down the vale and o'er the hills
Ustica's every echo fills.

The Gods, their bard caressing,
     With kindness treat:
They've fill'd my house with blessing—
     My country-seat,
Where Plenty voids her loaded horn,
Fair Tyndaris, pray come adorn!

From Sirius in the zenith,
     From summer's glare,
Come, where the valley screeneth,
     Come, warble there
Songs of the hero, for whose love
Penelope and Circe strove.

Nor shall the cup be wanting,
    So harmless then,
To grace that hour enchanting
    In shady glen.
Nor shall the juice our calm disturb,
Nor aught our sweet emotions curb?

    Fear not, my fair one! Cyrus
        Shall *not* intrude,
    Nor worry thee desirous
        Of solitude,
Nor rend thy innocent robe, nor tear
The garland from thy flowing hair.

                Francis Sylvester Mahony

A Dialogue Betwixt Horace and Lydia

Odes III, 9

HORACE

While, *Lydia,* I was lov'd of thee,
    Nor any was preferr'd 'fore me
To hug thy whitest neck: Then I,
The Persian King liv'd not more happily.

LYDIA

While thou no other didst affect,
Nor *Cloe* was of more respect;
Then *Lydia,* far-fam'd *Lydia,*
I flourish't more then Roman *Ilia.*

HORACE

Now *Thracian Cloe* governs me,
Skilfull i' th' Harpe, and Melodie:
For whose affection, *Lydia,* I
(So Fate spares her) am well content to die.

LYDIA

My heart now set on fire is
By *Ornithes* sonne, young *Calaïs;*
For whose commutuall flames here I
(To save his life) twice am content to die.

HORACE

Say our first loves we sho'd revoke,
And sever'd, joyne in brazen yoke:
Admit I *Cloe* put away,
And love againe love-cast-off *Lydia?*

LYDIA

Though mine be brighter then the Star;
Thou lighter then the Cork by far:
Rough as th' *Adratick sea,* yet I
Will live with thee, or else for thee will die.

Robert Herrick

The Reconciliation: A Modern Version

Odes III, 9

HORACE

What time I was your one best bet
    And no one passed the wire before me,
Dear Lyddy, I cannot forget
    How you would—yes, you would—adore me.
To others you would tie the can;
    You thought of me with no aversion
In those days I was happier than
    A Persian.

LYDIA

Correct. As long as you were not
  So nuts about this Chloe person,
Your flame for me burned pretty hot—
  Mine was the door you pinned your verse on.
Your favorite name began with L,
  While I thought you surpassed by no man—
Gladder than Ilia, the well-
    Known Roman.

HORACE

On Chloe? Yes, I've got a case;
  Her voice is such a sweet soprano;
Her people come from Northern Thrace;
  You ought to hear her play piano.
If she would like my suicide—
  If she'd want me a dead and dumb thing,
Me for a glass of cyanide,
    Or something.

LYDIA

Now Calaïs, the handsome son
  Of old Ornitus, has *me* going;
He says I am his honey bun,
  He's mine, however winds are blowing;
I think that he is awful nice,
  And if the gods the signal gave him,
I'd just as lieve die once or twice
    To save him.

HORACE

Suppose I'm gone on you again,
  Suppose I've got ingrown affection
For you; I sort of wonder, then,
  If you'd have any great objection.

Suppose I pass this Chloe up
And say: "Go roll your hoop, I'm rid o' ye!"
Would that drop sweetness in your cup?
    Eh, Lydia?

LYDIA

Why, say—though he's fair as a star,
    And you are like a cork, erratic
And light—and though I know you are
    As blustery as the Adriatic,
I think I'd rather live with you
    Or die with you, I swear to gracious.
So I will be your Mrs. Q.
    Horatius.

Franklin P. Adams

We Loved of Yore

Odes III, 26

We loved of yore, in warfare bold,
    Nor laurelless. Now all must go:
Let this left wall of Venus show
The arms, the tuneless lyre of old.

Here let them hang, the torches cold,
    The portal-bursting bar, the bow,
        We loved of yore.

But thou, who Cyprus sweet dost hold,
    And Memphis free from Thracian snow,
    Goddess and queen, with vengeful blow,
Smite,—smite but once that pretty scold
        We loved of yore.

Austin Dobson

Lastly to Venus

Odes IV, 1

V *enus,* againe thou mov'st a warre
   Long intermitted, pray thee, pray thee spare:
I am not such, as in the Reigne
Of the good *Cynara* I was: Refraine,
   Sower Mother of sweet Loves, forbeare
To bend a man now at his fiftieth yeare
   Too stubborne for Commands, so slack:
Goe where Youths soft intreaties call thee back.
   More timely hie thee to the house,
With thy bright Swans, of *Paulus Maximus:*
   There jest, and feast, make him thine host,
If a fit livor thou dost seeke to toast;
   For he's both noble, lovely, young,
And for the troubled Clyent fyl's his tongue,
   Child of a hundred Arts, and farre
Will he display the Ensignes of thy warre,
   And when he smiling finds his Grace
With thee 'bove all his Rivals gifts take place,
   He will thee a Marble Statue make
Beneath a Sweet-wood Roofe, neere *Alba Lake:*
   There shall thy dainty Nostrill take
In many a Gumme, and for thy soft eares sake
   Shall Verse be set to Harpe and Lute,
And *Phrygian* Hau'boy, not without the Flute.
   There twice a day in sacred Laies,
The Youths and tender Maids shall sing thy praise:
   And in the *Salian* manner meet
Thrice 'bout thy Altar with their Ivory feet.
   Me now, nor Wench, nor wanton Boy,
Delights, nor credulous hope of mutuall Joy,
   Nor care I now healths to propound;
Or with fresh flowers to girt my Temple round.
   But, why, oh why, my *Ligurine,*

Flow my thin tears, downe these pale cheeks of mine?
Or why, my well-grac'd words among,
With an uncomely silence failes my tongue?
Hard-hearted, I dreame every Night
I hold thee fast! but fled hence, with the Light,
Whether in *Mars* his field thou bee,
Or *Tybers* winding streames, I follow thee.

Ben Jonson

Witches, Hags, and other Abhorrences

In contrast to the suave and graceful odes on love-making and the charms of women, this section of ten poems might be called a book of invectives. Only three of these vinegarish pieces have a place among the Odes. The remaining seven are all early poems, one taken from the first book of the Satires and the other six from the Epodes. At the beginning of his literary career Horace indulged in a vehemence of dislike which he outgrew as he mellowed with age. The first satire of the second book is a considered defense of his work against the critics who had accused him of being too savage in his diatribes.

The charge is certainly not justified by the good-natured banter (Satires I, 8) that Horace first composed about a supposed witch whom he called Canidia. But the account of how the garden-god Priapus frightened away the midnight hags from Maecenas' new park on the Esquiline was succeeded by a horrible picture of the witches torturing a boy by slow starvation in order that they may brew a potent love-drink from his entrails. Possibly this poem brought threats of retaliation. A third Canidia poem takes the form of a mock apology, in which Horace speaks in his own person and the sorceress replies. The witch is mentioned again in the poet's vigorous complaint against a dish too highly seasoned with garlic.

The theme of the faded courtesan is one that François Villon has made his own, but he was anticipated by Horace in the three odes associated with this group of invectives. Two similar poems, altogether too foul-mouthed to quote, were included among his Epodes.

At the end of the group come three epodes attacking men whom the poet for various reasons disliked, a former slave who had risen to a post of high command in the navy, a libeler who had attacked someone in Horace's circle, and especially a certain poetaster named Maevius. Horace's farewell to him, wishing him every possible disaster on a sea voyage, is a little masterpiece of its kind. It is the direct antithesis of the ode (I, 3) which entreats the gods to guard well the precious life of Virgil as he sets sail for Greece.

Priapus and the Witches

Satires I, 8

A fig-tree log I used to be;
  The carpenter long considered these
Two things to make of useless me:
Priapus, or a stool of ease;
But finally settled on the god.
So godlike now with my right hand
I guard from thieves this bit of land,
Or fright them off with this red rod
Projecting from my ungainly groin;
A reed above my head is bound
To scare off birds that would purloin
Tidbits from this new garden ground.

In old days carcasses of slaves,
Dragged rudely from their narrow lairs
And borne by hirelings to their graves,
Here rested from their wretched lot
With all the refuse of the town.
Here among paupers you might find
The spendthrift Nomentanus, dead,
Likewise Pantolabus the clown.
A boundary pillar marked the spot:
"Frontage, three thousand feet," it read,
"Three hundred deep," with words designed
To save the burying ground from heirs.

137

Now property on the Esquiline
Has quite recovered from the slump:
It's healthy; people take the air
Along the sunny rampart, where
The dismal view they used to see
Was of a boneyard and a dump.
Prowlers no longer trouble me,
But once let fitful moonlight shine
When Luna bares her beauteous face,
And witches vex me worse than thieves;
They plague men's souls with drugs and spells,
And much my guardian spirit grieves
To hear their midnight songs and yells
And not to drive them from this place;
Nothing that I can threaten curbs
Their search for bones and baneful herbs.

I've seen (even I, the garden god)
The witch Canidia flitting round,
Swathed in black cloak, with feet unshod,
And shrouded in disheveled hair;
Beside her Sagana, her dam,
Piercing the air with owlish cries.
Horribly pale their faces were!
First they began to tear the ground
With talons, and a black ewe-lamb
Rent all to pieces with their teeth;
The dark blood filled the trench beneath
That ghosts might drink and make replies,
Uttering prophecies. This done
They took a puppet wrought of wool
And one of wax; the woolen one
Was larger, fashioned of a size
To daunt the weaker shape of wax,
Which like a suppliant, pitiful,
Cringed as if sentenced to the axe.
Then one witch summoned Hecate,
And one Tisiphone the dire,

While hell-hounds crept about and snakes;
The shrinking moon you now might see
Behind tall tombs hiding her fire
That such iniquities should be!

If any lying word I've said,
May crows' white droppings foul my head!
Get thief Voranus, Julius too,
And Pediatia, he who makes
Puddles, and let me be their jakes!

Would you hear more, most strange, most true?
How ghosts, when Sagana spoke, would mow
And gibber echoes sad and shrill,
And how the witches on the sly
Buried a wolf's beard in the ground
With tooth of spotted snake, and how
Fire from the waxen man blazed high,
And I was frightened fit to kill
At each ungodly sight and sound.
But quick to get revenge was I,
For bango! like a bladder burst,
Sudden my fig-wood buttock split,
Exploding in a cough reversed.
It makes me chuckle just to tell:
You should have seen them run for it!
Canidia lost the teeth she wore,
And Sagana's towering head-dress fell,
As scattering herbs and magic charms
A filthy litter from their arms,
Back into town those witches tore.

George F. Whicher

The Orgy

Epode 5

W^{hat}, O ye gods, who from the sky
    Rule earth and human destiny,
What means this coil? And wherefore be
These cruel looks all bent on me?
Thee by thy children I conjure
If at their birth Lucina pure
Stood by; thee by this vain array
Of purple, thee by Jove I pray,
Who views with anger deeds so foul,
Why thus on me like stepdame scowl,
Or like some wild beast, that doth glare
Upon the hunter from its lair?"

As thus the boy in wild distress
Bewail'd, of bulla stripp'd and dress,
So fair, that ruthless breasts of Thrace
Had melted to behold his face,
Canidia, with dishevell'd hair
And short crisp vipers coiling there,
Beside a fire of Colchos stands,
And her attendant hags commands
To feed the flames with fig-trees torn
From dead men's sepulchres forlorn,
With dismal cypress, eggs rubb'd o'er
With filthy toads' envenom'd gore,
With screech-owl's plumes, and herbs of bane,
From far Iolchos fetch'd and Spain,
And fleshless bones by beldam witch
Snatch'd from the jaws of famish'd bitch.
And Sagana, the while, with gown
Tucked to the knees, stalks up and down,
Sprinkling in room and hall and stair
Her magic hell-drops, with her hair

Bristling on end, like furious boar,
Or some sea-urchin wash'd on shore;
Whilst Veia, by remorse unstay'd,
Groans at her toil, as she with spade
That flags not digs a pit, wherein
The boy imbedded to his chin,
With nothing seen save head and throat,
Like those who in the water float,
Shall dainties see before him set,
A maddening appetite to whet,
Then snatched away before his eyes,
Till famish'd in despair he dies;
That when his glazing eyeballs should
Have closed on the untasted food,
His sapless marrow and dry spleen
May drug a philtre-draught obscene.
Nor were these all the hideous crew,
But Ariminian Folia, too,
Who with unsatiate lewdness swells,
And drags by her Thessalian spells
The moon and stars down from the sky,
Ease-loving Naples vows, was by;
And every hamlet round about
Declares she was, beyond a doubt.

Now forth the fierce Canidia sprang,
And still she gnaw'd with rotten fang
Her long sharp unpared thumb-nail. What
Then said she? Yea, what said she not?

"O Night and Dian, who with true
And friendly eyes my purpose view,
And guardian silence keep, whilst I
My secret orgies safely ply,
Assist me now, now on my foes
With all your wrath celestial close!
Whilst, stretch'd in soothing sleep, amid
Their forests grim the beasts lie hid,

May all Suburra's mongrels bark
At yon old wretch, who through the dark
Doth to his lewd encounters crawl,
And on him draw the jeers of all!
He's with an ointment smear'd, that is
My masterpiece. But what is this?
Why, why should poisons brew'd by me
Less potent than Medea's be,
By which, for love betray'd, beguiled,
On mighty Creon's haughty child
She wreaked her vengeance sure and swift,
And vanish'd, when the robe, her gift,
In deadliest venom steep'd and dyed,
Swept off in flame the new-made bride?
No herb there is, nor root in spot
However wild, that I have not;
Yet every common harlot's bed
Seems with some rare Nepenthe spread,
For there he lives in swinish drowse,
Of me oblivious, and his vows!
He is, aha! protected well
By some more skilful witch's spell!
But, Varus, thou, (doom'd soon to know
The rack of many a pain and woe!)
By potions never used before
Shalt to my feet be brought once more.
And 'tis no Marsian charm shall be
The spell that brings thee back to me!
A draught I'll brew more strong, more sure,
Thy wandering appetite to cure;
And sooner 'neath the sea the sky
Shall sink, and earth upon them lie,
Than thou not burn with fierce desire
For me, like pitch in sooty fire!"

On this the boy by gentle tones
No more essay'd to move the crones,

But wildly forth with frenzied tongue
These curses Thyestean flung.
"Your sorceries, and spells, and charms
To man may compass deadly harms,
But heaven's great law of Wrong and Right
Will never bend before their might.
My curse shall haunt you, and my hate
No victim's blood shall expiate.
But when at your behests I die,
Like the Fury of the Night will I
From Hades come, a phantom sprite—
Such is the Manes' awful might.
With crooked nails your cheeks I'll tear
And, squatting on your bosoms, scare
With hideous fears your sleep away!
Then shall the mob, some future day,
Pelt you from street to street with stones,
Till falling dead, ye filthy crones,
The dogs and wolves and carrion fowl,
That make the Esquiline their prowl,
In banquet horrible and grim
Shall tear your bodies limb from limb,
Nor shall my parents fail to see
That sight—alas, surviving me!"

Sir Theodore Martin

Poet and Witch

Epode 17

HORACE

Well, I surrender; to your skill I bow,
And humbly pray, by Proserpine below,
By Dian never lightly to be moved,
And by the books of incantation proved

Of virtue stars to call down from the sky,
Canidia, at length your spells let lie,
Let go, let go, turn back the speeding wheel!

Was not old Nereus' grandson moved to heal
King Telephus who dared 'gainst him to range
His Mysian troops, and darts with him exchange?
The valiant Hector's corse, delivered o'er
To dogs and vultures, Trojan matrons bore
To Ilios and anointed, when the king
Had left the walls, himself, alas, to fling
At obdurate Achilles' feet. The crew
Ulysses toilworn led their limbs withdrew
At Circe's will, from bristly hides and hard;
Then mind and voice returned, and their regard
Its former dignity resumed. For you
Whom sailor-men and pedlars so adore,
I've suffered punishment enough and more.

My youthful vigor's gone, my modest hue
Has left my bones with ghastly skin o'erlaid;
My hair with essences of yours is greyed.
My sufferings allow me no respite;
Night presses day, and day too presses night,
Nor is it in my power to ease the strain
Upon my lungs for sighing all in vain.
Therefore, poor wretch, I must at last admit
What I too hastily denied before,
That Sabine charms disturb the breast, and fit
Are Marsian spells one's head in twain to split.
There now! What want you from me more?

O Earth, O Sea! I burn as burnt before;
Nor Hercules besmeared with Nessus' blood,
Nor fervid Aetna's flame inflaring flood;
But you a Colchian poison-worship glow,
Until the winds contemptuous me shall blow

As dust and ashes. What the end? To die?
Or what do you propose as penalty?
Speak, speak! The penalty you fix I'll pay
I pledge my honor, ready to defray,
Whether a hundred steers you may require,
Or choose the flattery of a lying lyre.

Yes, modest, honest, you shall have your station
Among the stars, a golden constellation.
Castor and Pollux, angered at the shame
Cast upon Helen, prayers yet overcame,
And to the poet they restored his sight,
Which had been taken from him. So do you,
For well you can, remove this frenzy quite,
You, sullied by no stains to forbears due,
Nor ancient hag experienced to explore
The ninth-day ashes of the buried poor.
A kindly soul you are. Your hands are clean,
And Pactomeius is your son, I ween.
Yours is the blood with which the sheets are red
Whene'er the patient springs robust from bed.

CANIDIA

Why pour your plaints into unheeding ears?
Not rocks more deaf to naked mariners
The wintry ocean pounds with rollers high.
Shall you reveal and flout Cotytto's rites,
Free Cupid's mysteries, and vengeance fly?
Shall you who pontiff to our orgies came
When celebrated on the Esquilian heights,
Unpunished fill the city with my name?
What good to me to empty money-bags
Into the laps of wise Pelignian hags?
What good a swifter poison to prepare?

For you a doom more lingering than you car
To hope awaits. An irksome life for you,

Poor wretch, shall be protracted, with the view
That you may ever suffer tortures new.
The treacherous father of a treacherous son,
Tantalus, Pelops' sire, who never won
The rich elusive banquet, craves respite;
Respite Prometheus to the vulture chained;
And respite Sisyphus whose rock ne'er gained
A resting place upon the mountain's height:
The laws of Jupiter forbid. And so
Shall you one time desire to leap below
From some high tower; another time your breast
With Noric sword to pierce; and sadly pressed
With heartache wearisome a noose you'll tie
About your neck, but seek in vain to die.
Then, mounted on your hated neck, I'll ride
And spurn the earth in my triumphant pride.
Shall I who have the power, as well you know
Through prying, life and feeling to bestow
On waxen images, and pluck from heaven
The moon by incantations—I who even
Can raise the dead though burnt in fire,
And duly mix the potions of desire—
Shall I the issues of my art bewail
Because on you its force has chanced to fail?

Alexander Falconer Murison

A Counterblast against Garlic

Epode 3

May the man who has cruelly murdered his sire—
      A crime to be punished with death—
Be condemned to eat garlic till he shall expire
Of his own foul and venomous breath!

What stomachs these rustics must have who can eat
　This dish that Canidia made,
Which imparts to my colon a torturous heat,
　And a poisonous look, I'm afraid.

They say that ere Jason attempted to yoke
　The fire-breathing bulls to the plough
He smeared his whole body with garlic,—a joke
　Which I fully appreciate now.
When Medea gave Glauce her beautiful dress,
　In which garlic was scattered about,
It was cruel and rather low-down, I confess,
　But it settled the point beyond doubt.

On thirsty Apulia ne'er has the sun
　Inflicted such terrible heat;
As for Hercules' robe, although poisoned, 't was fun
　When compared with this garlic we eat!
Maecenas, if ever on garbage like this
　You express a desire to be fed,
May Mrs. Maecenas object to your kiss,
　And lie at the foot of the bed!

Roswell Martin Field

To a Faded Beauty

Odes I, 25

More rarely now the wanton boys
　Beat on your shutters closed, with noise
Enough to banish sleep. The door
　Opens no more,

So prompt of old. A lover now
Less and less often clamours, "How,

While I the night-long vigil keep,
  Can Lydia sleep?"

You in your turn, the scorn of men,
Shall weep in some lone alley, when
The North-wind sings a louder tune
  At change of moon,

While baffled lust, and hot desire
Which mads the breeding mares, shall fire
Your festered heart, and you in vain
  Shall then complain

That boys, who love the ivy-sheen
And prize the myrtle's deeper green,
To th' Eastern wind, drear winter's friend,
  Sere leaves commend.

Hugh MacNaghten

To Be Quite Frank

Odes III, 15

Your conduct, naughty Chloris, is
  Not just exactly Horace's
    Ideal of a lady
    At the shady
      Time of life;
You mustn't throw your soul away
On foolishness, like Pholoë—
    Her days are folly-laden—
    She's a maiden,
      You're a wife.

Your daughter, with propriety,
May look for male society,
    Do one thing and another
    In which mother
        Shouldn't mix;
But revels Bacchanalian
Are—or should be—quite alien
    To you a married person,
    Something worse'n
        Forty-six!

Yes, Chloris, you cut up too much,
You love the dance and cup too much,
    Your years are quickly flitting—
    To your knitting
        Right about!
Forget the incidental things
That keep you from parental things—
    The World, the Flesh, the Devil,
    On the level,
        Cut 'em out!

Franklin P. Adams

To Lyce

Odes IV, 13

The gods have heard, O Lyce! heard my prayer—
    The gods have heard—and thou art old!
And yet thou still wouldst fain be counted fair;
    With wine and laughter bold

Thy tipsy quavering voice full often seeks
By song to waken soft Desire.
But Love lurks now in Chia's tender cheeks,
    Young mistress of the lyre!

Ever unsated, still Love flits away
From aged, withered oaks like thee;
No wrinkled face like thine can bid him stay
    Thy faded charms to see.

Thy Coan purple never can restore—
Nor gems of price—those days again
Which once fast-flying Time hath reckoned o'er
    In records all too plain.

Where now hath fled thy charm? thy beauty where?
Thy comely grace? What now is left
Of her—of her—who, love in every air,
    Me of myself bereft?

For—after Cinara;—fate to thee was kind:
Wide-famed, with Welcome in thy face.
But few the years the gods to her assigned;
    Yet kept thee in thy place,

To be the aged raven's withered peer,
That ardent youths may now behold
Thy burnt-out torch, and flout with many a jeer
    The ashes stale and cold.

George Meason Whicher

The Upstart

Epode 4

As wolves by nature disagree
    With lambs, so I base wretch with thee;
Whose sides and legs do still retain
The marks of whips and servile chain.

Though of vast riches vainly proud,
A rascal still thou art allow'd:
When with six ells of gown in tail,
The holy way in state you trail,
Do you not hear the sneering boys
Insult you with incessant noise?
"There goes the dog, with whipping flay'd,
Till ev'ry bailiff loath'd his trade!
What num'rous acres now he ploughs,
What pomp and equipage he shews,
Sits foremost at the play in spite
Of Otho's laws, a worthy knight.
In vain our navies fight for peace,
And chace the pirates from the seas,
While such a villain has a share,
Or claims a glory in the war!"

John Parke

To a Bully

Epode 6

You, blatant coward that you are,
    Upon the helpless vent your spite.
Suppose you ply your trade on me;
Come, monkey with this bard, and see
    How I'll repay your bark with bite!

Ay, snarl just once at me, you brute!
    And I shall hound you far and wide,
As fiercely as through drifted snow
The shepherd dog pursues what foe
    Skulks on the Spartan mountain-side.

The chip is on my shoulder—see?
    But touch it and I'll raise your fur;
I'm full of business, so beware!
For, though I'm loaded up for bear,
    I'm quite as like to kill a cur!

Eugene Field

A Pleasant Voyage for Maevius

Epode 10

Under an evil star she slips,
    Accompanied by my hate;
She reels, unluckiest of ships,
    With him, her stinking freight.

Do not forget, O southwest wind,
    To lash her sides with waves,
Till Maevius sees, before, behind,
    Nothing but yawning graves.

Litter the sea, till on it lie
    These oars and tattered ropes;
And make the breakers tower as high
    As mountains on his hopes.

Let not one friendly star appear,
    Let even days be dark;
So that he'll fare as calm and clear
    —As Ajax' impious bark.

Ah, how the mariners will sweat!
    How Maevius will pale!
As weeping, woman-like and wet,
    He prays to stop the gale.

I too shall pray! And if a rock
Receive his mangled form,
The choicest ewe-lamb of the flock
I'll offer to the storm.

Louis Untermeyer

The Golden Mean

U nder this heading are grouped Horace's moral odes. *Aurea mediocritas,* the Golden Mean of the Stoics, did not imply a negative attitude, but the practice of a determined moderation in all things. A dynamic restraint has been the philosophy of true gentlemen in all ages, but in the sixteenth century especially, at the height of the English Renaissance, the ode (II, 10) in which Horace asserted the central tenet of his creed came to be a watchword of the humanists. It was translated by the court poet of Henry VIII, the ill-fated Earl of Surrey, in what appears to be the earliest rendering of any Horatian poem in English. Toward the close of the century it was again translated by Queen Elizabeth's courtier, the renowned Sir Philip Sidney, author of the *Arcadia.* Today the efforts of Surrey and Sidney seem awkward in comparison with the polished version of the same ode written by William Cowper.

Avoid extremes, maintain a balanced judgment and a serene mind. This theme is constantly sounded in Horace's verses, and from them it has been transferred to other literatures. The poetry of England's "Augustan Age" is charged with the Horatian spirit. On the basis of one of the moral odes (III, 29) Dryden wrote a florid paraphrase which has almost the force of an original poem, and Pope in his avowed imitations of Horace strove not without success to reproduce in English the Roman poet's philosophy as well as his conciseness and grace.

A corollary of the doctrine of moderation was the distaste for wealth, pomp, and display, an attitude more easily cultivated in the study than in the market place. A tiny ode (I, 38), hardly more than an exercise in versification on the theme of simplicity, has proved inexhaustibly attractive to translators. It appears below in seven different versions, none of which quite catches the quality of the original. There follow half a dozen poems in which Horace develops the Stoic scorn of luxury. It has been remarked that some of these border on the perfunctory.

But there is nothing half-hearted about the group of six odes (III, 1-6) with which this section ends. These "Inaugural Odes" are often taken together as though they were parts of a single symphonic composition on the theme of "the grandeur that was Rome." They seem to be calculated to awaken admiration for the traditional Roman virtues, to promote reverence for the gods, and above all to identify the destiny of Rome with the power and glory of Augustus. They indicate how deeply Horace was moved to support the revival of morality and religion which the emperor inaugurated about 28 B.C.

Praise of Meane and Constant Estate

Odes II, 10

Of thy lyfe, Thomas, this compasse well mark:
Not aye with full sayles the hye seas to beat:
Ne by coward dred, in shonning stormes dark,
On shalow shores thy keel in peril freat.

Who so gladly halseth the golden meane,
Voyde of dangers aduisdly hath his home
Not with lothsom muck, as a den vncleane:
Nor palacelyke, wherat disdayn may glome.

The lofty pyne the great winde often riues:
With violenter swey falne turrets stepe:
Lightninges assault the hye mountains, and cliues.
A hart well stayd, in ouerthwartes depe,

Hopeth amendes: in swete, doth feare the sowre.
God, that sendeth, withdraweth winter sharp.
Now ill, not aye thus: once Phebus to lowre
With bow vnbent shall cesse, and frame to harp

His voyce. In straite estate appere thou stout:
And so wisely, when lucky gale of winde
All thy puft sailes shall fil, loke well about:
Take in a ryft: hast is wast, profe doth finde.

Henry Howard, Earl of Surrey

"Draw in Thy Swelling Sailes"

Odes II, 10

Y ou better sure shall live, not evermore
　　Trying high seas, nor while seas rage you flee.
Pressing too much upon ill harbourd shore.

The golden meane who loves, lives safely free
　　From filth of foreworne house, and quiet lives,
Releast from Court, where envie needes must be.

The windes most oft the hugest Pine-tree greeves:
　　The stately towers come downe with greater fall:
The highest hills the bolt of thunder cleeves:

Evill happes do fill with hope, good happes appall
　　With feare of change, the courage well preparde:
Fowle Winters as they come, away they shall.

Though present times and past with evils be snarde,
　　They shall not last: with Citherne silent muse,
Apollo wakes, and bow hath sometime sparde.

In hard estate with stowt shew valor use,
　　The same man still in whom wise doome prevailes,
In too full winde draw in thy swelling sailes.

Sir Philip Sidney

The Golden Mean

Odes II, 10

Receive, dear friend, the truths I teach,
  So shalt thou live beyond the reach
  Of adverse fortune's power;
Not always tempt the distant deep,
Nor always timorously creep
  Along the treacherous shore.

He that holds fast the golden mean
And lives contentedly between
  The little and the great
Feels not the wants that pinch the poor
Nor plagues that haunt the rich man's door,
  Imbittering all his state.

The tallest pines feel most the power
Of wintry blasts; the loftiest tower
  Comes heaviest to the ground;
The bolts that spare the mountain's side
His cloud-capt eminence divide,
  And spread the ruin round.

The well-informed philosopher
Rejoices with a wholesome fear,
  And hopes in spite of pain;
If Winter bellow from the north,
Soon the sweet Spring comes dancing forth,
  And Nature laughs again.

What if thine heaven be overcast?
The dark appearance will not last;
  Expect a brighter sky;

The God that strings the silver bow
Awakes sometimes the Muses too,
    And lays his arrows by.

If hindrances obstruct thy way,
Thy magnanimity display
    And let thy strength be seen;
But O! if Fortune fill thy sail
With more than a propitious gale,
    Take half thy canvas in!

William Cowper

The Man of Life Upright

Odes I, 22

The man of life upright,
    Whose guiltless heart is free
From all dishonest deeds
    And thought of vanity:

The man whose silent days
    In harmless joys are spent,
Whom hopes cannot delude
    Nor sorrow discontent:

That man needs neither towers
    Nor armour for defence,
Nor secret vaults to fly
    From thunder's violence.

He only can behold
    With unaffrighted eyes
The horrors of the deep
    And terrors of the skies.

Thus scorning all the cares
     That fate or fortune brings,
He makes the heaven his book,
     His wisdom heavenly things,

Good thoughts his only friends,
     His wealth a well-spent age,
The earth his sober inn
     And quiet pilgrimage.

Thomas Campion

On Serenity

Odes III, 29

Paraphrased in Pindarick Verse

I

Descended of an ancient Line,
     That long the *Tuscan* Scepter sway'd,
Make haste to meet the generous Wine,
     Whose piercing is for thee delay'd:
The rosie wreath is ready made;
     And artful hands prepare
The fragrant *Syrian* Oyl, that shall perfume thy hair.

II

When the Wine sparkles from a far,
     And the well-natur'd Friend cries, come away;
Make haste, and leave thy business and thy care:
     No mortal int'rest can be worth thy stay.

III

Leave for a while thy costly Country Seat;
　　And, to be Great indeed, forget
The nauseous pleasures of the Great:
　　Make haste and come:
Come, and forsake thy cloying store;
　　Thy Turret that surveys, from high,
The smoke, and wealth, and noise of *Rome;*
　　And all the busie pageantry
That wise men scorn, and fools adore:
Come, give thy Soul a loose, and taste the pleasures of the poor.

IV

Sometimes 'tis grateful to the Rich, to try
A short vicissitude, and fit of Poverty:
　　A savoury Dish, a homely Treat,
　　Where all is plain, where all is neat,
Without the stately spacious Room,
The *Persian* Carpet, or the *Tyrian* Loom,
Clear up the cloudy foreheads of the Great.

V

The Sun is in the Lion mounted high;
　　　　The *Syrian* Star
　　　　Barks from afar,
And with his sultry breath infects the Sky;
The ground below is parch'd, the heav'ns above us fry.
　　The Shepheard drives his fainting Flock
　　Beneath the covert of a Rock,
　　And seeks refreshing Rivulets nigh,
　　The *Sylvans* to their shades retire,
Those very shades and streams new shades and streams require,
And want a cooling breeze of wind to fan the raging fire.

VI

Thou, what befits the new Lord May'r,
And what the City Faction dare,
And what the *Gallique* arms will do,
And what the Quiverbearing foe,
Art anxiously inquisitive to know:
But God has, wisely, hid from humane sight
  The dark decrees of future fate;
  And sown their seeds in depth of night;
He laughs at all the giddy turns of State;
When Mortals search too soon, and fear too late.

VII

Enjoy the present smiling hour;
  And put it out of Fortunes pow'r:
The tide of bus'ness, like the running stream,
  Is sometimes high, and sometimes low,
A quiet ebb, or a tempestuous flow,
    And alwayes in extream.
  Now with a noiseless gentle course
  It keeps within the middle Bed;
  Anon it lifts aloft the head,
And bears down all before it with impetuous force:
    And trunks of Trees come rowling down,
    Sheep and their Folds together drown:
  Both House and Homested into Seas are borne;
  And Rocks are from their old foundations torn,
'And woods, made thin with winds, their scatter'd honours mourn.

VIII

Happy the Man, and happy he alone,
  He, who can call to day his own:
  He who, secure within, can say,
To morrow do thy worst, for I have liv'd to-day.

Be fair, or foul, or rain, or shine,
The joys I have possest, in spight of fate, are mine.
Not Heav'n it self upon the past has pow'r;
But what has been has been, and I have had my hour.

IX

Fortune, that with malicious joy
Does Man her slave oppress,
Proud of her Office to destroy,
Is seldome pleas'd to bless:
Still various, and unconstant still,
But with an inclination to be ill.
Promotes, degrades, delights in strife,
And makes a Lottery of life.
I can enjoy her while she's kind;
But when she dances in the wind,
And shakes the wings, and will not stay,
I puff the Prostitute away:
The little or the much she gave, is quietly resign'd:
Content with poverty, my Soul I arm;
And Vertue, tho' in rags, will keep me warm.

X

What is't to me,
Who never sail in her unfaithful Sea,
If Storms arise, and Clouds grow black;
If the Mast split, and threaten wreck?
Then let the greedy Merchant fear
For his ill gotten gain;
And pray to Gods that will not hear,
While the debating winds and billows bear
His wealth into the Main.
For me, secure from Fortunes blows
(Secure of what I cannot lose,)
In my small Pinnace I can sail,
Contemning all the blustring roar;
And running with a merry gale.

With friendly Stars my safety seek
Within some little winding Creek;
   And see the storm a shore.

John Dryden

Contentment

Odes II, 16

Ease is the weary merchant's prayer,
   Who ploughs by night the Aegean flood,
When neither moon nor stars appear,
   Or faintly glimmer through the cloud.

For ease the Mede with quiver graced,
   For ease the Thracian hero sighs;
Delightful ease all pant to taste,
   A blessing which no treasure buys.

For neither gold can lull to rest,
   Nor all a Consul's guard beat off
The tumults of a troubled breast,
   The cares that haunt a gilded roof.

Happy the man whose table shows
   A few clean ounces of old plate;
No fear intrudes on his repose,
   No sordid wishes to be great.

Poor short-lived things, what plans we lay!
   Ah, why forsake our native home,
To distant climates speed away?
   For self sticks close where'er we roam!

Care follows hard, and soon o'ertakes
   The well-rigged ship, the warlike steed;
Her destined quarry ne'er forsakes;
   Not the wind flies with half her speed.

From anxious fears of future ill
   Guard well the cheerful, happy Now;
Gild e'en your sorrows with a smile,
   No blessing is unmixed below.

Thy neighing steeds and lowing herds,
   Thy numerous flocks around thee graze,
And the best purple Tyre affords
   Thy robe magnificent displays.

On me indulgent Heaven bestowed
   A rural mansion, neat and small;
This lyre;—and as for yonder crowd,
   The happiness to hate them all.

                William Cowper

Simplicity
Odes I, 38

Boy, I hate their empty shows,
   Persian garlands I detest,
Bring me not the late-blown rose
   Lingering after all the rest:

Plainer myrtle pleases me
   Thus outstretched beneath my vine,
Myrtle more becoming thee,
   Waiting with thy master's wine.

                William Cowper

Fie on Eastern Luxury!

Odes I, 38

Nay, nay, my boy—'tis not for me,
 This studious pomp of Eastern luxury;
Give me no various garlands—fine
 With linden twine,
Nor seek, where latest lingering blows,
 The solitary rose.

Earnest I beg—add not with toilsome pain,
One far-sought blossom to the myrtle plain,
For sure, the fragrant myrtle bough
 Looks seemliest on thy brow;
Nor me mis-seems, while, underneath the vine,
Close interweaved, I quaff the rosy wine.

Hartley Coleridge

A Victorian Paraphrase

Odes I, 38

Dear Lucy, you know what my wish is,—
 I hate all your Frenchified fuss:
Your silly entrees and made dishes
 Were never intended for us.
No footman in lace and in ruffles
 Need dangle behind my arm-chair;
'And never mind seeking for truffles,
 Although they be ever so rare.

But a plain leg of mutton, my Lucy,
   I prithee get ready at three:
Have it smoking, and tender and juicy,
   And what better meat can there be?
And when it has feasted the master
   'Twill amply suffice for the maid;
Meanwhile I will smoke my canaster
   And tipple my ale in the shade.

William Makepeace Thackeray

The Preference Declared

Odes I, 38

Boy, I detest the Persian pomp;
   I hate those linden-bark devices;
And as for roses, holy Moses!
   They can't be got at living prices!
Myrtle is good enough for us,—
   For *you,* as bearer of my flagon;
For *me,* supine beneath this vine,
   Doing my best to get a jag on!

Eugene Field

Persicos Odi: Pocket Version

Odes I, 38

Davus, I detest
   Persian decoration;
Roses and the rest,
Davus, I detest.

Simple myrtle best
  Suits our modest station;—
Davus, I detest
  Persian decoration.

Austin Dobson

Myrtle for Two

Odes I, 38

Persian flummery—
    Boy, how I hate it!
Not with linden bark
Let our wreaths be plaited;
And no roses, hark!
Late and last-of-summery.

Simple myrtle gather.
Myrtle, boy, is fitting
For a head like thine;
And while I drink, sitting
Shaded by the vine,
Myrtle suits me, rather.

George F. Whicher

Chicago Analogue

Odes I, 38

I do not share the common craze
    For food with jazzy singers;
Boy, tell me not of cabarets,
Where the late loophound lingers.

A glass of home brew cool and clear
  Wets down my home-cooked victuals;
So long as I can have my beer,
  I'll gladly miss the skittles.

Keith Preston

Money Is Not to Keep
Odes II, 2

Yes, you deservedly despise
    The wealth that use ne'er taught to shine,
That rusting in the coffer lies
  Like ore yet buried in the mine;
For gold, my friend, no lustre knows
But what a wise well-tempered use bestows.

Thee, Proculeius! distant days
  Will bless, and make thy virtues known,
Conspiring tongues will sound thy praise,
  A father's love to brethren shown:
Transcendent worth, like thine will fly
On Fame's unflagging pinions through the sky.

A monarch far more potent he
  Who subject keeps his wayward soul;
Who lives from sordid avarice free,
  And dares each fiercer lust control,
Than he whose universal sway
Wide earth's extremes, her East and West obey.

That sensual self-indulgent wretch
  Whose skin the panting dropsy strains,
Still must the watery languor stretch,
  And only Temperance ease his veins;
So growing wealth prompts new desire,
And Fortune's breeze but fans the wasting fire.

The Persian hails the public voice
 Decked with the crown that Cyrus wore;
But virtue sanctions not the choice;
 She calls Phraates blessed no more:
Can tyrant hands, defiled with sin,
The fair, the spotless mind of virtue win?

Virtue, their rule perverse, shall own
 Which bliss to wealth and grandeur leaves,
From virtue he and he alone,
 The wreath and diadem receives
Who dares the glittering heap pass by
With steadfast mien and unreverted eye.

Gilbert Wakefield

No Gilded Roof Is Mine

Odes II, 18

No gilded roofe, nor Ivorie Fret,
 For splendor in my house is set;
Nor are beames from Hymettia sought,
To lye a-thwart rich Columnes, brought
From Affrick; nor I heire unknowne,
Make Attalus his wealth, mine owne.
No honest Tenants wives you see,
Laconian Purples weave for mee:
A loyall heart, and ready vaine
Of wit I have, which doth constraine
Rome's richest men to seeke the love
Of me, though poore: Nor Gods above
Doe I invoke for larger store;
Nor of *Maecenas* aske I more.
To me my single Sabine field,
Sufficient happinesse doth yeeld.

One day thrust's on another fast,
And new Moones to the wane doe hast.
When death (perhaps) is neere at hand,
Thou fairest Marbles dost command
Be cut for use, yet dost neglect
Thy Grave, and houses still erect:
Nay would'st abridge the vast Sea's shore,
Which lowdly doth at Baiae rore:
Enrichéd little, lesse content,
With limits of the Continent.
Why often pull'st thou up the bounds,
T' enlarge the Circuit of thy grounds,
Encroaching farre from confines knowne,
To make the neighbouring field thine own?
The Husband, wife, and sordid brood,
With ancient Household Gods, that stood
In quiet peace, must be expell'd:
Yet is not any mansion, held
For the rich Land-lord so assur'd
As deepe in Hell to be immur'd.
Then whither doe you further tend?
Th' indifferent Earth, an equall friend,
As willingly opens her wombe,
For Begger's grave, as Princes Tombe.
Gold could of *Charon* not obtaine,
To bear *Prometheus* back againe.
Proud *Tantalus,* and all his stock,
Death, with the bands of Fate doth lock:
And call'd, or not call'd ready stands,
To free the poore from painfull bands.

Sir Thomas Hawkins

Choose Moderate Riches

Odes III, 16

The lone grey tower on Argos' mountain shore,
    The faithful watch-dog at the midnight door;
Safe in their guard imprisoned love had slept,
Her baffled suitors youthful Danaë wept.
But, with rich bribes, the laughing gods betrayed
The yielding guardian and the enamoured maid,
Through arméd satellites and walls of stone,
Gold wings his flight, resistless though alone.

Ah! who the wiles of womankind hath tried?
By gold, the priest, the blameless augur died.
Mark Philip's march! The obedient cities fall,
Ope the wide gates, and yield the embattled wall.
To gold each petty tyrant sank a prey,
King after king confessed its powerful sway.
The war-worn veteran oft his trophies sold;
And venal navies owned the power of gold.

Enlarging wealth increasing wishes share,
The gods have cursed the miser's hoard with care:
To modest worth are choicest blessings sent;
Heaven loves the humble virtues of content.
Far from the rich the poet loves to dwell,
And share the silence of the hermit's cell.

The wild brook, babbling down the mountain's side;
The chestnut copse that spreads its leafy pride;
The garden plot that asks but little room,
The ripening cornfield, and the orchard's bloom;
These simple pleasures, trust me, are unknown
To the rich palace or the jewelled throne;
The wealthy lords of Afric's wide domain
Would spurn my lowly roof and bounded plain.

Cold are the Sabine hills! hives not for me
Its hoarded nectar the Calabrian bee.
Here no rich vines their amber clusters rain,
Not mine the fleece that decks the Gallic plain.
Yet want, for once, avoids a poet's door,
Content and grateful, can I ask for more?
But should thy bard seek ampler means to live,
Patron and friend, thy liberal hand would give.

What if increasing wealth withholds its shower?
If the rich widow guards her jealous dower?
Then, wiser, learn the effect is still the same,
From humbler wishes and contracted aim,
More wealthy thou than if thy lands could join
All Phrygia's harvests to the Lydian mine;

Not want alone surrounds the opening door,
For pride and avarice are ever poor;
Delusive hope and wild desire combined
Feed with vain thoughts the hunger of the mind.
But blest is he, to whom indulgent Heaven
Man's happiest state, enough not more, has given.

John Mitford

Wealth Encroaches

Odes II, 15

Soon to the plough our palaces will spare
Few acres: giant fish-ponds everywhere
Large as Lake Lucrine will be sights to see:
Elms will give place to planes unwedded, bare

Of clinging vines. The violets, myrtles, all
That idly feeds the nostrils, shall enthral
     The sense, mid olive groves fruit-bearing once,
Now taught to look so green and grow so tall.

The laurel leaves shall keep the pleasaunce cool
Where once the strong suns glowed. Not such the rule
     Of Romulus and Cato, when the beard
Proclaimed the man; not such the ancient school.

Small was each private income long ago
But public wealth was great. No portico
     Measured by ten-foot rods, for private use,
That faced the shady North and shunned the glow.

Their laws forbade to leave the former ways
And scorn the chance-cut turf, though bidding raise
     Town-buildings at the public cost, and hew
New stone for temples, in the ancient days.

Hugh MacNaghten

To the Covetous

Odes III, 24

Though thou, of wealth possessed,
     Beyond rich Ind's, or Araby's the blest,
Shouldst with thy palace keeps
Fill all the Tuscan and Apulian deeps,
     If Fate, that spoiler dread,
Her adamantine bolts drive to the head,
     Thou shalt not from despairs
Thy spirit free, nor loose thy head from death's dark snares.

The Scythians of the plains
More happy are, housed in their wandering wains,
    More blest the Getan stout,
Who not from acres marked and meted out
    Reaps his free fruits and grain:
A year, no more, he rests in his domain,
    Then, pausing from his toil,
He quits it, and in turn another tills the soil.

    The guileless stepdame there
The orphan tends with all a mother's care;
    No dowried dame her spouse
O'erbears, or trust the sleek seducer's vows;
    Her dower a blameless life,
True to her lord, she shrinks an unstained wife
    Even from another's breath;
To fall is there a crime, and there the guerdon death!

    Oh for the man, would stay
Our gory hands, our civil broils allay!
    If on his statues he
Sire of the Common-weal proclaimed would be,
    Let him not fear to rein
Our wild licentiousness, content to gain
    From after-times renown,
For ah! while Virtue lives, we hunt her down,
    And only learn to prize
Her worth, when she has passed for ever from our eyes!

    What boots it to lament,
If crime be not cut down by punishment?
    What can vain laws avail,
If life in every moral virtue fail?
    If nor the clime, that glows,
Environed round by fervid heats, nor snows
    And biting Northern wind,
Which all the earth in icy cerements bind,
    The merchant back can keep,
And skilful shipmen flout the horrors of the deep?

Yes! Rather than be poor,
What will not mortals do, what not endure?
  Such dread disgrace to shun,
From virtue's toilsome path away we run.
  Quick, let us, 'mid the roar
Of crowds applauding to the echo, pour
  Into the Capitol,
Or down into the nearest ocean roll
  Our jewels, gems, and gold,
Dire nutriment of ills and miseries untold!

  If with sincere intent
We would of our iniquities repent,
  Uprooted then must be
The very germs of base cupidity,
  And our enervate souls
Be braced by manlier arts for nobler goals!
  The boy of noble race
Can now not sit his steed, and dreads the chase,
  But wields with mastery nice
The Grecian hoop, or even the law-forbidden dice!

  What marvel, if the while
His father, versed in every perjured wile,
  For vilest private ends
Defrauds his guests, his partners, and his friends,
  His pride, his only care,
To scramble wealth for an unworthy heir!
  They grow, his ill-got gains,
But something still he lacks, and something ne'er attains!

Sir Theodore Martin

Of Greatness

Odes III, 1

I

H ence, ye Profane; I hate ye all;
 Both the Great, Vulgar, and the small.
To Virgin Minds, which yet their Native whiteness hold,
Not yet Discolour'd with the Love of Gold,
 (That Jaundice of the Soul,
Which makes it look so Guilded and so Foul)
To you, ye very Few, these truths I tell;
The Muse inspires my Song, Heark, and observe it well.

II

We look on Men, and wonder at such odds
 'Twixt things that were the same by Birth;
We look on Kings as Giants of the Earth,
These Giants are but Pigmeys to the Gods.
 The humblest Bush and proudest Oak,
Are but of equal proof against the Thunder-stroke.
Beauty, and Strength, and Wit, and Wealth, and Power
 Have their short flourishing hour;
 And love to see themselves, and smile,
And joy in their Preeminence a while;
 Even so in the same Land,
Poor Weeds, rich Corn, gay Flowers together stand;
Alas, Death Mowes down all with an impartial Hand.

III

And all you Men, whom Greatness does so please,
 Ye feast (I fear) like *Damocles:*
 If you your eyes could upwards move,
(But you (I fear) think nothing is above)

You would perceive by what a little thread
   The Sword still hangs over your head.
No Title of Wine would drown your cares;
No Mirth or Musick over-noise your feares.
The fear of Death would you so watchfull keep,
As not t' admit the Image of it, sleep.

IV

Sleep is a God too proud to wait in Palaces
And yet so humble too as not to scorn
   The meanest Country Cottages;
   His Poppey grows among the Corn.
The Halcyon sleep will never build his nest
   In any stormy breast.
     'Tis not enough that he does find
     Clouds and Darkness in their Mind;
     Darkness but half his work will do.
'Tis not enough; he must find Quiet too.

V

The man, who in all wishes he does make,
   Does onely Natures Counsel take.
That wise and happy man will never fear
   The evil Aspects of the Year;
Nor tremble, though two Comets should appear;
He does not look in Almanacks to see,
   Whether he Fortunate shall be;
Let *Mars* and *Saturn* in th' Heavens conjoyn,
And what they please against the World design,
   So *Jupiter* within him shine.

VI

If of your pleasures and desires no end be found,
God to your Cares and Fears will set no bound.
   What would content you? Who can tell?
Ye fear so much to lose what you have got,
   As if you lik'd it well.

Ye strive for more, as if ye lik'd it not.
  Go, level Hills, and fill up Seas,
Spare nought that may your wanton Fancy please
  But trust Me, when you have done all this,
Much will be Missing still, and much will be Amiss.

Abraham Cowley

Roman Virtues
Odes III, 2

The Roman youth should learn to gladly bear
    The toils of war, sharp penury, and care,
Should on his gallant steed with mighty spear
Bear, through the Parthian ranks, dismay and fear;
That when from her high tower the foeman's queen
Or some ripe maiden his brave deeds has seen,
They both may tremble lest their love should dare
To meet the lion-champion riding there,
Who makes, mid carnage fell, his dreadful way
Through the thick masses of the foes' array.

How blest is he who for his country dies,
Since death pursues the coward as he flies!
The youth in vain would fly from Fate's attack;
With trembling knees, and Terror at his back;
Though Fear should lend him pinions like the wind,
Yet swifter Fate will seize him from behind.

Virtue repulsed, yet knows not to repine;
But shall with unattainted honour shine;
Nor stoops to take the staff, nor lays it down,
Just as the rabble please to smile or frown.

Virtue, to crown her favourites, loves to try
Some new unbeaten passage to the sky;
Where Jove a seat among the gods will give
To those who die, for meriting to live.

Next faithful Silence hath a sure reward;
Within our breast be every secret barr'd!
He who betrays his friend, shall never be
Under one roof, or in one ship, with me:
For who with traitors would his safety trust,
Lest with the wicked, Heaven involve the just?
And though the villain 'scape a while, he feels
Slow vengeance, like a bloodhound, at his heels.

Anonymous, lines 1-10
Jonathan Swift

Ilium Fuit, Roma Est

Odes III, 3

The man of firm and righteous will,
    No rabble, clamorous for the wrong,
No tyrant's brow, whose frown may kill,
    Can shake the strength that makes him strong:
Not winds, that chafe the sea they sway,
    Nor Jove's right hand, with lightning red:
Should Nature's pillared frame give way,
    That wreck would strike one fearless head.
Pollux and roving Hercules
    Thus won their way to Heaven's proud steep,
'Mid whom Augustus, couch'd at ease,
    Dyes his red lips with nectar deep.
For this, great Bacchus, tigers drew
    Thy glorious car, untaught to slave

In harness: thus Quirinus flew
    On Mars' wing'd steeds from Acheron's wave,
When Juno spoke with Heaven's assent:
    "O Ilium, Ilium, wretched town!
The judge accurst, incontinent,
    And stranger dame have dragg'd thee down.
Pallas and I, since Priam's sire
    Denied the gods his pledged reward,
Had doomed them all to sword and fire,
    The people and their perjured lord.
No more the adulterous guest can charm
    The Spartan queen: the house forsworn
No more repels by Hector's arm
    My warriors, baffled and outworn:
Hush'd is the war our strife made long:
    I welcome now, my hatred o'er,
A grandson in the child of wrong,
    Him whom the Trojan priestess bore.
Receive him, Mars! the gates of flame
    May open: let him taste forgiven
The nectar, and enrol his name
    Among the peaceful ranks of Heaven.
Let the wide waters sever still
    Ilium and Rome, the exiled race
May reign and prosper where they will:
    So but in Paris' burial-place
The cattle sport, the wild beasts hide
    Their cubs, the Capitol may stand
All bright, and Rome in warlike pride
    O'er Media stretch a conqueror's hand.
Aye, let her scatter far and wide
    Her terror, where the land-lock'd waves
Europe from Afric's shore divide,
    Where swelling Nile the corn-field laves—
Of strength more potent to disdain
    Hid gold, best buried in the mine,
Than gather it with hand profane,
    That for man's greed would rob a shrine.

Whate'er the bound to earth ordain'd,
   There let her reach the arm of power,
Travelling, where raves the fire unrein'd,
   And where the storm-cloud and the shower.
Yet, warlike Roman, know thy doom,
   Nor, drunken with a conqueror's joy,
Or blind with duteous zeal, presume
   To build again ancestral Troy.
Should Troy revive to hateful life,
   Her star again should set in gore,
While I, Jove's sister and his wife,
   To victory led my host once more.
Though Phoebus thrice in brazen mail
   Should case her towers, they thrice should fall,
Storm'd by my Greeks: thrice wives should wail
   Husband and son, themselves in thrall."
—Such thunders from the lyre of love!
   Back, wayward Muse! refrain, refrain
To tell the talk of gods above,
   And dwarf high themes in puny strain.

John Conington

The Voice of the Muse
Odes III, 4

Descend from Heaven, Calliope, and bring
   The long-drawn breath of thy melodious flute,
Or the wild throbbings of Apollo's lute;
Or with uplifted voice th' heroic anthem sing!
Is this some phantom sound that mocks mine ear?—
   'Tis she, the Muse! I hear, I hear
   The voice Divine. Methinks I rove
Listening her song within some sacred grove
Where through the branches summer breezes play
And caverned streams in silence glide away.

Child of the Muse, on Voltur's steep
Beyond Apulia's bounds I strayed:
Wearied with sport I sank to sleep:—
Doves, dear to legendary lore,
From woodlands far fresh flowers and leaflets bore,
And hid th' unconscious infant 'neath their shade.

In myrtle wrapped, close-veiled in bay,
Secure from snakes and savage beasts I lay,
A fearless babe protected from on high
Sleeping the innocent sleep of infancy;
A miracle to all that dwell
On Acherontia's mountain citadel,
Or rich Ferentum's plain, or Bantia's forest dell.
Uplifted by the Muses I explore
The arduous summits of rude Sabine hills:
Yours, and forever yours, I gaze
On cool Praeneste, and the rills
Of Tibur upturned to the noontide rays,
And liquid Baiae on the Tyrrhene shore.
So dear to you, Immortal Nine, is he,
The bard who loves your fountains and your song,
Philippi's headlong flight bore him unharmed along:
You saved him from the falling tree
And that Sicilian sea
Where Palinurus' cliff blackens the stormy wave.
Fearless with you my feet would brave
Wild Bosphorus, Assyria's burning sand,
Inhospitable Britain, and the land
Of warlike Concans nursed on horses' blood,
Gelonia's quivered hordes, and Scythia's frozen flood.

Caesar with warlike toils opprest
In your Pierian cavern finds his rest,
His weary legions citizens once more;
While you, rejoicing pour
Into his heart mild counsels from on high,
Counsels of mercy, peace and thoughtful piety.

We know how Jove,
Who rules with just command
Cities and Nations, and the Gods above,
The solid Earth, the Seas, and, down beneath,
The ghostly throng that haunts the realms of death,
Launched the swift thunder from his outstretch hand,
And down to darkness hurled the Titans' impious band.

Shuddered the Strong One at the sight
One moment, when with giant might
That Earth-born generation strove
To pile up Pelion on Olympus' height,
And scale the Heavens: but what bested
Rhoetus, or Mimas, or Typhoeus dread,
Porphyrion's towering form the Gods defying,
Enceladus who as a spear could wield
Uprooted pines? Amazed they fled
Pallas with her echoing shield,
Queen Juno, Vulcan burning for the fight,
And him who by Castalia lying
Bathes in the sacred fount his unbound hair;
That God whose shoulders ever bear
The Cynthian bow; Phoebus who honours still
Delos, his natal isle, and Lycia's bosky hill.

Power, reft of wisdom, falls by its own weight:
Wisdom, made one with strength, th' Immortals bless,
And evermore exalt: they hate
Tyrannous force untempered, pitiless.

Diana's virgin dart
Drank the dark blood of Orion's heart;
And hundred-handed Gyas met his doom
Crushed 'neath the darkness of a living tomb.
Earth, heaped upon those buried Portents, mourns
Her monstrous sons. The insatiate flame
Forever under Etna burns,
Yet ne'er consumes its quivering frame:

Forever feasts the vulture brood
Remorseless upon Tityos' blood;
The lover base, Pirithous, complains
Forever 'neath the weight of his three hundred chains.

Sir Stephen Edward De Vere

The True Roman Temper

Odes III, 5

Jove reigns in heaven, the thunder seems to say,
And we believe: but Jove is far away:
  On earth Augustus shall be held divine,
When Briton and dread Persian own his sway.

What? Has the soldier, one whom Crassus led,
Wooed a strange wife, grown old, with honour dead,
  (O! Roman Senate and the ancient ways!)
Among the kinsmen armed of her he wed,

A Marsian or Apulian, and become
A Median slave, forgetting hearth and home
  And sacred shields, and Vesta's deathless flame,
While Jupiter still reigns and Rome is Rome!

This, this it was foresaw the counsel sage
Of Regulus, forbidding to engage
  The state to shameful terms, and tracing doom
From such a precedent to th' unborn age,

Unless the Roman Senate left to die
Unpitied, men who had surrendered: "I
  Have seen our standards in the Punic shrines
And arms," he said, "from Roman infantry

Seized without bloodshed: I have lived to see
Hands bound behind the backs that once were free,
  Their gates wide open, and the fields that once
We ravaged, tilled in all security.

More bold, forsooth, the soldier goes to fight
When ransomed. Will your loss of gold make bright
  Their soil of honour? Wool recovers not,
Once steeped in dye, the wonder of its white,

And once 'tis lost true valour has no mind
In men degenerate again to find
  A dwelling place. Then, only then, when fights
Freed from the close-meshed nets the timid hind,

Will he be brave, and live to humble high
Carthage in war, who knew his enemy
  Faithless and yielded, let his arms be bound,
Endured the coward's brand and feared to die.

This man took war for peace, and did not know
To what a Roman armed his life should owe!
  Foul shame is ours, while Carthage rises high
From Italy's dishonoured overthrow."

They tell us how as outcast from his race
He put aside his own true wife's embrace
  And little children, looking grimly down
Still with the stern set purpose on his face,

Till, championing a matchless precedent,
He nerved the wavering peers to give consent
  That he, amid the mourning of his friends,
Should pass in haste to glorious banishment.

Full well the Roman knew he should not lack
The thousand tortures of the Punic rack,
  Yet through opposing kinsmen forced a way
And brushed aside the crowds that called him back,

As though, the court's last sentence given, he
From all the weary suits of clients free
   Were leaving Rome for green Venafrum, or
Tarentum, Lacedaemon's colony.

Hugh MacNaghten

Honor the Gods

Odes III, 6

Those ills your ancestors have done,
   Romans! are now become your own:
      And they will cost you dear,
      Unless you soon repair
The falling temples, which the gods provoke,
And statues, sullied yet with sacrilegious smoke.
Propitious Heaven, that raised your fathers high
      For humble grateful piety,
      (As it rewarded their respect)
   Hath sharply punished your neglect.
   All empires on the gods depend,
Begun by their command, at their command they end
Let Crassus' ghost and Labienus tell
How twice, by Jove's revenge, our legions fell,
      And with insulting pride,
Shining in Roman spoils, the Parthian victors ride.
      The Scythian and Egyptian scum
      Had almost ruined Rome,
   While our seditions took their part,
Filled each Egyptian sail, and winged each Scythian dart.
      First these flagitious times
      (Pregnant with unknown crimes)
   Conspire to violate the nuptial bed,
      From which polluted head

Infectious streams of crowding sins began,
And through the spurious breed and guilty nation ran.
  Behold a fair and melting maid
  Bound 'prentice to a common trade:
Ionian artists, at a mighty price,
Instruct her in the mysteries of vice,
What nets to spread, where subtle baits to lay,
And, with an early hand, they form the tempered clay.
  'Tis not the spawn of such as these,
That dyed with Punic blood the conquered seas,
  And quashed the stern Aeacides;
Made the proud Asian monarch feel
How weak his gold was against Europe's steel;
  Forced e'en dire Hannibal to yield,
And won the long disputed world, at Zama's fatal field.
  But soldiers of a rustic mould,
  Rough, ready, seasoned, manly, bold;
  Either they dug the stubborn ground,
Or, through hewn woods, their weighty strokes did sound;
  And after the declining sun
Had changed the shadows, and their task was done,
Home with their weary team they took their way,
And drowned in friendly bowls the labour of the day.
    Time sensibly all things impairs;
    Our fathers have been worse than theirs;
    And we than ours; next age will see
    A race more profligate than we,
With all the pains we take, have skill enough to be.

Wentworth Dillon, Earl of Roscommon

The One Inexorable Thing

Death to Horace was an everlasting exile from joy. Whether or not he believed in the classical fables of an afterlife in some dim underworld, it was clear to him that substantial pleasures came to an end as each man entered the realm of shadows. Beyond our brief mortal span was nothing but dust and dreams.

Like other finely tempered natures Horace resigned himself to the inevitable without blinking. "What we are powerless to cure must be borne with patience." Dignity demands that we accept whatever is to be without too much curiosity about the future. Yet without indulging in any mental evasions the tragic brevity of life may be turned to use for poetry. Horace sounded very memorably the note of pagan melancholy. Time flies—earth and its pleasures are slipping from us—enjoy, oh, enjoy the passing hour—for it is all we have. *Carpe diem,* "harvest today." One may hear the same plangent cry echoed down the centuries in Omar's

> *Ah, make the most of what we yet may spend*
> *Before we too into the Dust descend;*

in Ronsard's

> *Cueillez, cueillez vostre jeunesse;*

in Herrick's

> *Gather ye rosebuds while ye may;*

and in many another line, since the pagan melancholy is not confined to pagans.

The passing of man to return no more can be given added poignance by contrast with the perpetual recurrence of day and night, the seasons, and the objective facts of nature. So Catullus wrote:

> *Suns that set may rise again,*
> *But we, our little light expended,*
> *In darkness never to be ended*
> *Always and always shall remain.*

and Keats, hearing the nightingale's unvarying song, exclaimed:

> *Thou wast not born for death, immortal bird!*
> *No hungry generations tread thee down.*

One of the supreme expressions in all literature of this fundamental sadness of mortal life is Horace's *Diffugere Nives* (Odes IV, 7), which Dr. Samuel Johnson has translated with robust vigor and A. E. Housman with delicate appreciation of its imperishable loveliness. By looking straight at the fact of death and not seeking to abate its terrors, Horace achieved a depth of lyrical emotion unequaled in any other section of his poetry.

To Leuconoë

Odes I, 11

Seek not, O Maid, to know,
  (Alas! unblest the trying!)
When thou and I must go.

No lore of stars can show
What shall be, vainly prying,
Seek not, O Maid, to know.

Will Jove long years bestow?—
Or is't with this one dying,
That thou and I must go;

Now,—when the great winds blow,
And waves the reef are plying?—
Seek not, O Maid, to know.

Rather let clear wine flow,
On no vain hope relying;
When thou and I must go

Lies dark;—then be it so.
Now,—now, churl Time is flying;
Seek not, O Maid, to know
When thou and I must go.

Austin Dobson

Carpe Diem
Odes I, 11

Pry not in forbidden lore,
Ask no more, Leuconoë,
How many years—to you?—to me?—
The gods will send us
Before they end us;
Nor, questing, fix your hopes
On Babylonian horoscopes.

Learn to accept whatever is to be:
Whether Jove grant us many winters,
Or make of this the last, which splinters
Now on opposing cliffs the Tuscan sea.

Be wise; decant your wine; condense
Large aims to fit life's cramped circumference.
We talk, time flies—you've said it!
Make hay today,
Tomorrow rates no credit.

George F. Whicher

Consolation to Valgius
Odes II, 9

'Tis not always the fields are made rough by the rains,
'Tis not always the Caspian is harried by storm;
Neither is it each month in the year
That the ice stands inert on the shores of Armenia;

Nor on lofty Garganus the loud-groaning oaks
Wrestle, rocked to and fro with the blasts of the north,
  Nor the ash-trees droop widowed of leaves.
    O my friend, O my Valgius, shall grief last forever?

Yet thy heart in its yearning forever pursues
The loved and lost Mystes; the star of the eve,
  And the sunrise which chases the star,
    Find thy love still lamenting the loss of thy Mystes.

But the old man, who three generations lived through,
Did not for Antilochus mourn all his years:
  Nor for Troilus, nipped in his bloom,
    Flowed forever the tears of his parents and sisters.

Wean thy heart then at last from these memories too soft,
Let us chant the fresh trophies our Caesar has won,
  Linking on, to the nations subdued,
    Bleak Niphates all ice-locked, the Mede's haughty river,

Now submissively humbling the crest of its waves;
While the edict of Rome has imprisoned the Scyths,
  In the narrow domain of their steppes,
    And the steed of each rider halts reined at the borders.

                              Lord Lytton

The Ghost of Archytas to the Sailor

Odes I, 28

SAILOR

Archytas, wanderer of the deep,
    And o'er the innumerable sand,
A little want thereof doth keep
Upon the lone Matinian strand.

Nor may it now avail thee aught,
That thou hast compassed earth and sky—
And e'en celestial mansions sought—
In thine appointed hour to die.

ARCHYTAS

Yes, Pelops' sire, the guest of Gods,
And old Tithonus passed away—
And Minos, dear in Jove's abodes
Is now, like me, but common clay.

And in the dim Tartarean shades,
Again dismissed to mournful night,
Pythagorus' ransomed spirit fades—
That mighty judge of truth and right;

Aye! though he marked the very shield
His former self, Euphorbus bore,
When, battling on the Trojan field,
He died, a thousand years before.

But one long night awaits us all—
One path by all must trodden be—
The soldier's doom, in fight to fall—
The sailor's, in the insatiate sea.

Together old and young go forth,
Together lie their mingled graves,—
Me, too, the cold tempestuous North
Has whelmed beneath Illyrian waves.

But, Sailor! do not thou, unkind,
Refuse a little sand to spread
Of all that's swept by Ocean's wind,
O'er these unburied bones and head.

So, when the stormy East shall move,
Upon the rough Hesperian sea,
Although it strip Venusia's grove,
Thy bark shall safe and sheltered be.

And many a rich and noble freight
From every port where winds may sweep,
Thy pious hand shall still await
By Neptune wafted o'er the Deep.

But if, regardless of the Dead,
Thou hastenest cold and careless by—
The Gods' avenging anger dread,
And scorn from every honest eye.

It will not long delay thee here—
Thrice scatter earth above my frame,
This last, sad, pious rite revere,
And thou mayst hurry on, the same.

Henry Howard Brownell

To an Ambitious Friend

Odes II, 11

Omit, omit, my simple friend,
   Still to inquire how parties tend,
Or what we fix with foreign powers.
If France and we are really friends,
And what the Russian Czar intends,
   Is no concern of ours.

Us not the daily quickening race
Of the invading populace
Shall draw to swell that shouldering herd.

Mourn will we not your closing hour,
Ye imbeciles in present power,
  Doomed, pompous, and absurd!

And let us bear, that they debate
Of all the engine-work of state,
Of commerce, laws, and policy,
The secrets of the world's machine,
And what the rights of man may mean,
  With readier tongue than we.

Only, that with no finer art
They cloak the troubles of the heart
With pleasant smile, let us take care;
Nor with a lighter hand dispose
Fresh garlands of this dewy rose,
  To crown Eugenia's hair.

Of little threads our life is spun,
And he spins ill, who misses one.
But is thy fair Eugenia cold?
Yet Helen had an equal grace,
And Juliet's was as fair a face,
  And now their years are told.

The day approaches, when we must
Be crumbling bones and windy dust;
And scorn us as our mistress may,
Her beauty will no better be
Than the poor face she slights in thee,
  When dawns that day, that day.

Matthew Arnold

Returning Spring

Odes I, 4

Hard Winter melts; the welcome Spring again
    Comes back, and in her train
The West wind, and the laid-up keels once more
    Are launched from the dry shore.
No longer do the herds the stalls desire
    Nor husbandman his fire;
The meadows that but now were white with frost
    Their pallid hues have lost.
In dance, by Cytherean Venus led,
    With the moon overhead,
Joined with the Nymphs the sister Graces beat
    The earth with rhythmic feet,
While at the Cyclops' ponderous forge the light
    Makes swarthy Vulcan bright.
Now round the tresses that with unguents shine
    Green myrtles we may twine,
Or flowers with which from icy fetters freed
    Earth garnishes the mead.
Now is the time to make in shady groves
    The offerings Pan loves,
Whether he may demand a lamb or bid
    Oblation of a kid.
Pale death before them stalks impartially,
    Whether the portals be
Of peasant or of prince—hovel or tower—
    Alike all feel his power.
O happy Sestius! Life's little span
    Forbids long hope to man;
Thy sunny day impending night invades,
    Thee wait the fabled Shades,
And Pluto's narrow house; where, once thou go,
    No more by lucky throw

Of dice wilt thou in banquet hall recline
King of the realms of wine;
No tender Lycidas will love inspire,
Whose charms thou dost admire,—
Whom rival youths regard with jealous eye,
And maids will by and by.

John Osborne Sargent

The Stoic

Odes II, 3

An equal mind, when storms o'ercloud,
Maintain, nor 'neath a brighter sky
Let pleasure make your heart too proud,
O Dellius, Dellius! sure to die,
Whether in gloom you spend each year,
Or through long holydays at ease
In grassy nook your spirit cheer
With old Falernian vintages,
Where poplar pale, and pine-tree high
Their hospitable shadows spread
Entwined, and panting waters try
To hurry down their zigzag bed.
Bring wine and scents, and roses' bloom,
Too brief, alas! to that sweet place,
While life, and fortune, and the loom
Of the Three Sisters yield you grace.
Soon you must leave the woods you buy,
Your villa, wash'd by Tiber's flow,
Leave,—and your treasures, heap'd so high,
Your reckless heir will level low.
Whether from Argos' founder born
In wealth you lived beneath the sun,
Or nursed in beggary and scorn,

You fall to Death, who pities none.
One way all travel; the dark urn
　　Shakes each man's lot, that soon or late
Will force him, hopeless of return,
　　On board the exile-ship of Fate.

John Conington

Vision of Death

Odes II, 14

Swiftly, alas! O Postumus, Postumus,
　　Glide by the years in their feverish flight;
Age lingers never, nor heedeth our piety
　　Death in his conquering might.

E'en though in hundreds victims thou numberest,
　　Daily thy life from the grave to redeem,
Merciless, pitiless, Pluto still mocketh thee,
　　Lord of the turbulent stream.

Dark is that stream, yet all shall encounter it,
　　Drawn by a doom unchanging and sure;
None shall escape, be he pauper or potentate,
　　Prince or the veriest boor.

Vainly we shun grim War with its slaughtering,
　　Vainly the wave and the tempest's wild breath;
Vain is our fear of the blight of the eastern wind,
　　Laden with fever and death.

Soon to Cocytus, sullenly wandering
　　Down through the darkness, we too must descend,
One with the band ever wearily, hopelessly
　　Toiling with never an end.

Lands, home and loved ones, thou must abandon them,
Gardens and orchards that gladden thy way;
There shall no trees save the cypress funereal
Follow their lord of a day.

Worthier heirs thy wines shall be squandering,
Carefully guarded with bolt and with bar,
Recklessly wasting thy costliest vintages,
Flinging thy treasure afar.

Charles Ernest Bennett

Lament for Quintilius

Odes I, 24

Unshamed, unchecked, for one so dear
We sorrow. Lead the mournful choir,
Melpomene, to whom thy sire
Gave harp, and song-notes liquid-clear!

Sleeps He the sleep that knows no morn?
Oh Honour, oh twin-born with Right
Pure Faith, and Truth that loves the light,
When shall again his like be born?

Many a kind heart for Him makes moan;
Thine, Virgil, first. But ah! in vain
Thy love bids heaven restore again
That which it took not as a loan:

Were sweeter lute than Orpheus given
To thee, did trees thy voice obey;
The blood revisits not the clay
Which He, with lifted wand. hath driven

Into his dark assemblage, who
   Unlocks not fate to mortal's prayer.
   Hard lot! Yet light their griefs who bear
The ills which they may not undo.

Charles Stuart Calverley

Mortality

Odes IV, 7

The snow dissolv'd no more is seen,
   The fields, and woods, behold, are green,
The changing year renews the plain,
The rivers know their banks again,
The spritely Nymph and naked Grace
The mazy dance together trace.
The changing year's successive plan
Proclaims mortality to Man.
Rough Winter's blasts to Spring give way,
Spring yields to Summer's sovereign ray,
Then Summer sinks in Autumn's reign,
And Winter chils the World again.
Her losses soon the Moon supplies,
But wretched Man, when once he lies
Where Priam and his sons are laid,
Is naught but Ashes and a Shade.
Who knows if Jove who counts our Score
Will toss us in a morning more?
What with your friend you nobly share
At least you rescue from your heir.
Not you, Torquatus, boast of Rome,
When Minos once has fix'd your doom,
Or Eloquence, or splendid birth,
Or Virtue shall replace on earth.

Hippolytus unjustly slain
Diana calls to life in vain,
Nor can the might of Theseus rend
The chains of hell that hold his friend.

Samuel Johnson

Dust and Dreams

Odes IV, 7

The snows are fled away, leaves on the shaws
  And grasses in the mead renew their birth,
The river to the river-bed withdraws,
  And altered is the fashion of the earth.

The Nymphs and Graces three put off their fear
  And unapparelled in the woodland play.
The swift hour and the brief prime of the year
  Say to the soul, *Thou wast not born for aye.*

Thaw follows frost; hard on the heel of spring
  Treads summer sure to die, for hard on hers
Comes autumn with his apples scattering;
  Then back to wintertide, when nothing stirs.

But oh, whate'er the sky-led seasons mar,
  Moon upon moon rebuilds it with her beams;
Come *we* where Tullus and where Ancus are
  And good Aeneas, we are dust and dreams.

Torquatus, if the gods in heaven shall add
  The morrow to the day, what tongue has told?
Feast then thy heart, for what thy heart has had
  The fingers of no heir will ever hold.

When thou descendest once the shades among,
   The stern assize and equal judgment o'er,
Not thy long lineage nor thy golden tongue,
   No, nor thy righteousness, shall friend thee more.

Night holds Hippolytus the pure of stain,
   Diana steads him nothing, he must stay;
And Theseus leaves Pirithous in the chain
   The love of comrades cannot take away.

                         A. E. Housman

Conversations and Letters in Verse

If we may judge by the frequency with which quotations appear in medieval collections of epigrams and sententious sayings, the Satires and Epistles of Horace were about five times as popular during the Middle Ages as the Odes and Epodes. Today the shorter poems are far better known than the conversation pieces. The Epistles are charming models of urbane composition, and the Satires include many passages of autobiographical interest. The brilliant sketches of Priapus and the Witches (Satires I, 8) and of Horace plagued by an unwelcome companion (Satires I, 9) have lost nothing of their color in the lapse of two thousand years. But much of the substance of the longer poems is bound up with Roman customs and attitudes of mind which can be appreciated only after special study. Consequently the selection of Satires and Epistles for this book has been limited to a few representative specimens.

Roman satire—the word *satura* means a mixture or variety of things—originated in a sort of rustic farce, a native dramatic form which was superseded by regular drama after the Greek pattern. The early poets Ennius and Pacuvius composed *saturae* intended for reading rather than acting, but the man who stamped literary satire with his genius was Gaius Lucilius, a maternal uncle of Pompey the Great, who lived about a century before Horace. His satires are often minutely autobiographical, but contain also comments on friends and foes, the follies of the time, philosophy, religion, and literature, travels and adventures, eating, drinking, and the trivial events of life. Horace followed Lucilius in the general conception of his work, except that he considered that his attacks were aimed less at individuals than at the vices and unsocial attitudes of his age. His Satires were informal discussions of anything and everything that interested him.

Some of Horace's Epistles are letters in the true sense, invitations to dine, letters of inquiry, and one even a tactful letter of introduction. But the longer Epistles like the Satires tend toward a single type: the informal essay in verse. For both of them Horace used the word *sermones,* which may best be translated "chats." Possibly the moral Epistles are a shade more personal than the Satires, but the poet claimed that neither were addressed to the public at large. He considered that he was writing in dressing-gown and slippers for a small audience of his intimate friends, the "fit and few."

The general tone of these compositions has been perfectly caught by Alexander Pope in his Epistle to Dr. Arbuthnot and his more direct imitations of Horace. His paraphrase of The Country Mouse (Satires II, 6) is included in this section.

Good Birth—and What of It!

Satires I, 6

Of all the dwellers on Etruscan ground
    For somewhat Lydian ancestry renowned,
Maecenas, if we give to each his due,
There is no greater gentleman than you.
Though on maternal and paternal side
Your grandsires mighty legions used to guide,
Unlike the common run, a squinnied nose
You never will turn up at any of those
Whose forebears were unknown, nor even at me
Born of a father who had been set free.
A man must be freeborn, but otherwise
You don't go in for genealogies;
And what his father was, won't interest you.
You'll therefore be convinced that this is true;
Long years before the distant day and hour
When Tullius had come to regal power
Whose mother was a slave of low degree,
Many a man without much ancestry,
Leading a life of probity and worth,
Won ample honors, that belied his birth.
Laevinus, on the other hand, come down
From that Valerius of old renown
Who banished from the realm, Tarquin the Proud,
Could never, as the many have allowed,
Be any more expensive than one cent.
Voters, you know, are not intelligent.
Honors they give to men who have no merit,
The servile fools of halfwits who inherit

Titles, or whose patrician galleries
Are lined with forebears' waxen effigies
What part is proper then for us to play,
From all the vulgar herd so far away?
Only suppose the populace prefer
Such honors on Laevinus to confer
While Decius, the parvenu, they flout.
Suppose the censor moved to kick me out,
And I must be held up to public scorn
Because I had a father not freeborn.
I'd sure deserve the jam that I got in,
Not staying put inside of my own skin.
Forever chained to Glory's glittering car
Alike the vulgar and the nobles are.
So Tillius, what's the use, when yesterday
Your senatorial stripe was torn away,
To seek a tribune's office to attain,
So you can wear the purple once again?
Malicious envy only grows more rife,
Much less, if you retired to private life.
Who wants to stand in senatorial shoes
Is crazy: that will be his sole excuse,
When with black leather thongs his legs are dressed,
And broad the stripe let down upon his chest;
Continually he'll hear: "Who is that man?
Who was his father?" Barrus once began
To be infected with a strange disease;
And with a splendid shape desired to please.
Wherever he went the girls would then and there
Look over all his points with interest rare,
And ask about his face, calves, feet and teeth and hair.
So if a man will make a promise to
The voters, of big things that he will do
For City, Empire, Italy and the shrine
Of every god the Romans hold divine,
Those mortals all are bound to ask with care:
"Who was his father? Was the lady fair
Who bore him, flesh of flesh and bone of bone,

A woman no one else had ever known?
How dare you, son of a Syrus or a Damas
Or of a Dionysus, so to shame us?
Would you a Roman citizen throw down
From the Tarpeian Rock, you base born clown?
Or hand to Cadmus to be executed?"
"But Novius, my colleague so reputed,
Must park one seat behind me, when we see
The games. He's what my father used to be."
"And so you think yourself on this account
A Paulus or Messalla? What do you amount
To anyway? But he's the people's choice.
Novius has a mighty speaking voice.
For when two hundred trucks make an infernal noise,
And three large funerals come to swell the sound
In the great Forum, louder he'll resound;
Trumpets and horns alike his voice will drown.
Anyway, we're not going to let him down."
So now I will return again to me,
"Born of a father who had been set free."
Like rats they gnaw me, every slanderous knave,
"Born of a father who had been a slave."
And that's the way they now behave to me,
Maecenas, when we both good comrades be;
And that's the same old argument they made
Because a Roman legion once obeyed
Me for a Colonel, maybe rightly then;
But now I'll say it's something else again.
My former honor, all the world agrees
Could give a grouch to anyone you please.
But why should anyone be jealous now
Of you and me as friends; they must know how
Particular you are in making friends
Only of those with worthy aims and ends;
All base and crooked flattery is far
From you, who pick your friends for what they are.
So for our friendship, I could never say
Only a stroke of luck had come my way.

No happy chance bestowed you upon me,
But Virgil once, and best of all was he.
After him Varius; so it came to pass
When they had told you everything I was.
But when I came before you, face to face,
I hemmed and hawed, much to my own disgrace.
Like a small infant bashfully I came,
And more I could not say for very shame.
Not I a father's fame inherited;
I never rode upon a thoroughbred
Across the Satureian countryside;
I told you what I was; and you replied
Little, for that's your way; and off I pack.
And when nine months went by, you called me back,
And bade me to be numbered with your friends;
And this, I reckon, all the rest transcends,
That I should be found pleasing in your sight,
With your discernment of the wrong and right.
Me no paternal honors recommend;
But pure in life and heart, I am your friend.
And if my blemishes are slight and few,
But otherwise I'm naturally true,
As for a body shapely on the whole,
You might pick flaws, if spotted by a mole.
If none could really blame me to my hurt
For greed or any other kind of dirt,
If to a fancy house I never went,
But all my life was pure and innocent,
If I do say so, and to friends endeared,
My father was the reason. So he reared
Me. Poor he was. His paltry little field
Could scarcely a sufficient harvest yield;
Yet he refused to put me in the rule
Of Flavius, who ran the village school;
Where boys of big centurions used to go.
Big husky boys; who carried to and fro
On the left arm, the satchel and the slate.
The middle of each month, they shelled out eight

Coppers for payment. But my father dared
To bring his boy to Rome to be prepared,
A training any senator or knight
Would give his sons, if they were taught aright.
My dress, the slaves who followed me about,
If one could notice me in all that rout,
He'd think the pomp and circumstance was due
Alone to large ancestral revenue.
Father himself acted as bodyguard,
Not to be bribed by any man's reward.
He went to my instructors every day
About the school. There is no more to say.
Honorably my father saved for me
The flower of all the virtues, chastity,
Not only in the fact but in the name.
On me no breath of scandal ever came;
He never was afraid of anyone
Who told him he did wrong to give his son
A liberal education. Even if I
Earned but an auctioneer's small salary.
Or if a bill collector I'd remain,
As he was once, I never could complain.
For all this now, what praise can I bestow
On him, much greater than the thanks I owe?
Could I of such a father be inclined
Ever to be ashamed, in my right mind?
Some think they're smart, saying they're not to blame
For parents who had neither name nor fame.
I'll not defend myself in any way
Like that; and what I think and what I say
Will nothing have in common with that crowd.
If, after certain years had been allowed,
At Nature's call, we lived them over again
And other parents of a nobler strain
Each could select according to desire,
Whomever his ambition might require,
Such high and haughty honors I'd resign,
Content with what in former days were mine.

The crowd will call me crazy; you, maybe,
Pronounce me sane, when for the like of me
The fasces I refuse, and curule chair,—
Such crushing burdens, all unfit to bear.
If I desired to take a rustic trip
All by myself, I never more could slip
Out of the city. I should have to feed
A train of grooms and thoroughbreds. I'd need
A coach. But now, according to my due
I take a bobtailed mule for retinue.
And way down to Tarentum I can go
With him. My saddle bags will chafe below
His buttocks, while his rider sore must gall
His foreparts. But there's nobody to call
Me stingy, Tillius, as the gossips goad
You when you travel the Tiburtine road.
A praetor very niggardly behaves
Who on a journey only takes five slaves,
To carry for the hour when he would dine
A portable oven and a hamper of wine.
In that and in a thousand other ways,
Your Excellency, I can pass my days
Much more agreeably than you have done.
Whenever I want, I take a walk alone.
I bargain over cabbages and flour;
I ramble round the Circus at the hour
Of evening, where they gyp the people so;
And afterwards around the Forum go;
At fortune teller's booths I show my hand;
And last of all, once more at home I land.
Arrived I sup on scallions, potted pease
And pancakes made of meal and fried in grease;
Three boys will wait on me; a slab of white
Marble upholds two cups of measure right
For mixing of the water and the wine.
An inexpensive saltcellar is mine;
Pitcher and plate to pour libations there,
And both are of Campanian earthenware.

And so to bed, where worry dies aborning.
I need not get up early in the morning
To plead my clients' cases and to see
Marsyas' statue glowering down at me;
Inside the Forum; always frowning thus,
His face abhors the junior Novius
Who just behind his back a pawnshop keeps,
Open for business, while the city sleeps.
I'm up at ten to take a little walk,
Or read or write with no disturbing talk.
A rubdown then with olive oil, not that
Stolen from table lamps by nasty Nat;
And when the sun with penetrating rays
Reminds me to the bath to go my ways,
I keep away from Campus and the ball
Game. Afterwards my lunch is very small,
An empty stomach just enough to stay.
And so at home I pass the time away.
Desire for honor and the heavy strife
Of fell ambition cumber not my life;
But cheerfully I live and at my ease.
In such a life there is much more to please
Than if a quaestor grandfather were mine,
And father and my uncle all in line.

Henry Harmon Chamberlin

To Maecenas

On Patronage

Epistles I, 7

Pledged in the country but five nights to stay—
August is past, and lo! I still delay,
False to my word. But if, dear sir, you care
To see me in good plight and debonair,

That license which you grant me sick, I know
You'll not deny me fearing to be so,—
Now that pale Autumn marshals forth again
The undertaker with his rueful train,—
While each fond mother with distraction wild
Hangs o'er the pillow of her sickening child,—
While levees thronged and law-courts never still
Let loose the fever and unseal the will.
But when autumnal drought to winter yields
And drifting snows have bleached the Alban fields,
Down to the sea your poet will retire
To read in comfort couched beside the fire;
Anon, when zephyrs breathe and swallows sing,
To greet his patron with returning spring.
      Your kindness, sir, to me, is really kind;—
Not like the boons of some Calabrian hind
With fulsome zeal that will not be repressed
Forcing his pears upon the sated guest.
"Come, eat them, pray!"—"I've eaten all I would."
"Then pocket what you please."—"You're very good.
Your infant tribe would deem them no bad store.
I'm as obliged as if I took a score."
"Well, please yourself; but know, what you decline
Will fall ere night a portion to the swine."
      The spendthrift and the fool are so polite,
They give to others what they hate or slight;
And where love's seed is sown with hand so rude,
No wonder if the crop's ingratitude.
The good and wise, though anxious to uphold
True worth, yet wot that lupines are not gold.
For me, I ever shall be proud to raise
My worth in justice to my patron's praise:
But, would you have me never quit your side,
First give me back those locks whose jetty pride
Once clustered o'er my brow in gallant trim;—
Give back the well-strung nerve and vigorous limb;—
With that gay converse and those spirits light
That o'er the bowl deplored coy Cynara's flight.

A Fox's whelp one day half-famished stole
Into a corn-bin through a narrow hole;
Where having gorged his fill, he strove in vain
To squeeze his bloated carcase out again:
"Friend," cried a weazel near, "first mend your shape;
You entered lean, and lean you must escape."
Should Fortune ever, on this footing, call
Her favours back, I could resign them all;
Nor, capon-fed, with hypocritic air
Would I preach up the peasant's frugal fare;
Nor should the wealth of all Arabia please,
Taxed with the loss of liberty and ease.

Oft have you praised me as of modest views,
More prompt to laud your bounty than abuse;
Oft in your presence, nor less oft away,
As my liege-lord I've hailed your gentle sway.
Try me—and (though with thanks received) you'll find
Your gifts can be with cheerfulness resigned.
Well did Ulysses' son, as poets sing,
Thank for his proffered steeds the Spartan king:—
"The rocky island whence I drew my birth,
Albeit to me the loveliest spot on earth,
Nor stretched in plains nor rich in grassy food
Is ill-adapted for the equine brood:
Wherefore I would renounce, if you permit,
Those boons, good monarch! for yourself more fit."
Small things become the small: for me Rome's noise
And pomp imperial now present no joys,
Far more disposed to dream away the hours
In Tibur's peaceful shades or soft Tarentum's bowers.

Philippus, for his pleadings famed afar,
Alert and bold, returning from the Bar
About the hour of two one sultry day,
And now complaining that the length of way
Grew for his years too much, espied ('tis said)
A smug-faced cit beneath a barber's shed

Paring his nails with easy unconcern;—
Then called his lackey—"Boy, step in and learn
Who this may be—his family—his fame—
Where he resides—and what's his patron's name."
The lad (by name Demetrius) lacked not skill
Or promptness to despatch his master's will.
He flies—returns—informs him in a trice,
'Twas one Vulteius Mena, pure from vice,
Of humble means, by trade an auctioneer,
Who bustled to and fro to raise the gear,
Lounged when his daily toils were at an end,
Was fain to get, but not afraid to spend;—
Mixed with acquaintance of his own degree,
Had a fixed dwelling, and enjoyed with glee
The public shows; or, when his work was done,
In Mars's field at tennis would make one.
"Troth, I should like to know the wight; go, say
I should be glad he'd dine with me to-day."
Mena, the message heard, in mute surprise
Stares, and can scarce believe his ears and eyes;
Begs his devout acknowledgments,—in sum
Feels flattered and obliged, but cannot come.
"How! does the wretch then slight me?"—"Even so,
And through contempt or shyness answers, no."
Next morning, as Philippus strolls along,
He 'spies Vulteius to a tunic'd throng
Vending cheap wares, and having crossed the street,
Makes toward his client and is first to greet.
He, humbly bowing, pleads the ties of trade
And business, that he had not early paid
His compliments; ev'n now, in toils immersed,
Is shocked to think he had not hailed him first.
"On one condition be your pleas allowed—
Dine with me to-day."—"Sir, I shall be proud."
"Enough—you'll come at the ninth hour; till which
Go, ply your trade and labour to be rich."
The hour arrives—he goes—and having said
Some wisdom and some foolery, hies to bed.

Day after day when thus he kindly took
The flattering bait and nibbled round the hook,
A morning dangler now and constant guest;
What time the Latian festival gives rest
To wrangling law-courts, he's invited down
To see his patron's seat not far from town,
Perched in the chaise, he lauds in terms most high
The golden crops, green lawns, and Sabine sky.
Philippus, much diverted all the while,
Sees his scheme work and sees it with a smile,
Resolved with all chance pastime care to drown.
In short, seven thousand sesterces paid down,
With seven more proffered at an easy rate,
Tempt him to buy and farm a snug estate.
'Tis bought; and (not to spin my story out)
The smart cit drops into the rustic lout;—
He prattles of his tilth and vines—prepares
His elms—and launches in a sea of cares,
Stung to the quick with gain's delusive itch
And pining with the thirst of waxing rich.
Soon after (mark the change!) night-plunderers seize
His lambs; his she goats perish with disease;
Now blighted harvests mock his hopes; and now
The jaded ox drops dead beneath his plough.
Teased with his losses, cursing fortune's spite,
Snatching his nag at the mid hour of night,
Half-frantic to his patron's seat he goes,
Unshorn, with squalid garb that speaks his woes.
"How now!" Philippus cries, "Your looks are such,
I fear you drudge too hard and toil too much."
"Troth, patron! to this merit I've no claim;
Wretched I am, and that's my proper name.
Then oh! by all the ties of faith and love,
By all your boons, and by the powers above,
Kind sir! I do conjure you and implore,
Replace me in my pristine state once more."
      The moral of my tale is briefly this:
Let him who finds that he has changed amiss,

And that his promised joy turns out but pain,
With all convenient speed change back again!
'Tis a sound rule that each man has his pleasure,
And each should mete himself by his own measure.

Francis Howes

The Journey to Brundusium

Satires I, 5

'Twas a long journey lay before us
    When I and honest Heliodorus,
Who far in point of rhetoric
Surpasses every living Greek,
Each leaving our respective home,
Together sallied forth from Rome.
    First at Aricia we alight,
And there refresh and pass the night.
Our entertainment? rather coarse
Than sumptuous, but I've met with worse.
    Thence o'er the causeway soft and fair
To Appii Forum we repair.
But as this road is well supplied
(Temptation strong!) on either side
With inns commodious, snug, and warm,
We split the journey, and perform
In two days' time what's often done
By brisker travellers in one.
    Here rather chusing not to sup
Than with bad water mix my cup,
After a warm debate, in spite
Of a provoking appetite,

I sturdily resolve at last
To balk it, and pronounce a fast,
And in a moody humour wait,
While my less dainty comrades bait.
  Now o'er the spangled hemisphere
Diffus'd the starry train appear,
When there arose a desperate brawl;
The slaves and bargemen, one and all,
Rending their throats (have mercy on us!)
As if they were resolv'd to stun us.
"Steer the barge this way to the shore!"
"I tell you we'll admit no more!"
"Plague! will you never be content!"
Thus a whole hour at least is spent,
While they receive the several fares,
And kick the mule into his gears.
Happy, these difficulties past,
Could we have fall'n asleep at last!
But, what with humming, croaking, biting,
Gnats, frogs, and all their plagues uniting,
These tuneful natives of the lake
Conspir'd to keep us broad awake.
Besides, to make the concert full,
Two maudlin wights, exceeding dull,
The bargeman and a passenger,
Each in his turn essay'd an air
In honour of his absent fair.
At length the passenger, opprest
With wine, left off, and snor'd to rest.
The weary bargeman too gave o'er,
And hearing his companion snore,
Seiz'd the occasion, fix'd the barge,
Turn'd out his mule to graze at large,
And slept, forgetful of his charge.
  And now the sun, o'er eastern hill,
Discover'd that our barge stood still;

When one, whose anger vex'd him sore,
With malice fraught, leaps quick on shore,
Plucks up a stake; with many a thwack
Assails the mule and driver's back.
   Then slowly moving on, with pain,
At ten Feronia's stream we gain,
And in her pure and glassy wave
Our hands and faces gladly lave.
Climbing three miles, fair Anxur's height
We reach, with stony quarries white.
   While here, as was agreed, we wait,
Till, charg'd with business of the state,
Maecenas and Cocceius come
(The messengers of peace) from Rome;
My eyes, by wat'ry humours blear
And sore, I with black balsam smear.
At length they join us, and with them
Our worthy friend Fonteius came;
A man of such complete desert
Antony lov'd him at his heart.
   At Fundi we refus'd to bait,
And laugh at vain Aufidius' state;
A praetor now, a scribe before,
The purple border'd robe he wore,
His slave the smoking censer bore.
   Tir'd at Muraena's we repose
At Formia, sup at Capito's.
   With smiles the rising morn we greet;
At Sinuessa pleas'd to meet
With Plotius, Varius, and the bard
Whom Mantua first with wonder heard.
The world no purer spirits knows,
For none my heart more warmly glows.
Oh! what embraces we bestow'd,
And with what joy our breasts o'erflow'd!
Sure, while my sense is sound and clear,
Long as I live, I shall prefer

A gay, good-natur'd, easy friend,
To ev'ry blessing Heaven can send.
    At a small village, the next night,
Near the Vulturnus, we alight;
Where, as employ'd on state affairs,
We were supplied by the purvey'rs
Frankly at once, and without hire,
With food for man and horse, and fire.
    Capua next day betimes we reach,
Where Virgil and myself, who each
Labour'd with different maladies,
His such a stomach, mine such eyes,
As would not bear strong exercise,
In drowsy mood to sleep resort;
Maecenas to the tennis-court.
    Next at Cocceius' farm we're treated,
Above the Caudian tavern seated;
His kind and hospitable board
With choice of wholesome fare was stor'd.
    Now, O ye Nine, inspire my lays!
To nobler themes my fancy raise!
Two combatants, who scorn to yield
The noisy, tongue-disputed field,
Sarmentus and Cicirrus, claim
A poet's tribute to their fame;
Cicirrus of true Oscian breed,
Sarmentus, who was never freed,
But ran away; we don't defame him;
His lady lives, and still may claim him.
Thus dignified, in hardy fray
These champions their keen wit display;
And first Sarmentus led the way.
"Thy locks," quoth he, "so rough and coarse,
Look like the mane of some wild horse."
We laugh. Cicirrus, undismay'd,
"Have at you!" cries, and shakes his head.
" 'Tis well," Sarmentus says, "you've lost
That horn your forehead once could boast;

Since, maim'd and mangled as you are,
You seem to butt." A hideous scar
Improv'd, 'tis true, with double grace
The native horrors of his face.
Well, after much jocosely said
Of his grim front, so fiery red,
(For carbuncles had blotch'd it o'er,
As usual on Campania's shore)
"Give us," he cried, "since you're so big,
A sample of the Cyclops' jig!
Your shanks, methinks, no buskins ask,
Nor does your phyz require a mask."
To this Cicirrus: "In return,
Of you, Sir, now I fain would learn
When 'twas, no longer deem'd a slave,
Your chains you to the Lares gave?
For though a scrivener's right you claim,
Your lady's title is the same.
But what could make you run away,
Since, pygmy as you are, each day
A single pound of bread would quite
O'erpower your puny appetite?"
Thus jok'd the champions, while we laugh'd,
And many a cheerful bumper quaff'd.

To Beneventum next we steer,
Where our good host by over-care
In roasting thrushes lean as mice
Had almost fall'n a sacrifice.
The kitchen soon was all on fire,
And to the roof the flames aspire.
There might you see each man and master
Striving, amidst this sad disaster,
To save the supper—then they came
With speed enough to quench the flame.

From hence we first at distance see
Th' Apulian hills, well known to me,
Parch'd by the sultry western blast,
And which we never should have past,

Had not Trivicus, by the way,
Receiv'd us at the close of day.
But each was forc'd at entering here
To pay the tribute of a tear,
For more of smoke than fire was seen,
The hearth was pil'd with logs so green.

From hence in chaises we were carried
Miles twenty-four, and gladly tarried
At a small town, whose name my verse
(So barbarous is it!) can't rehearse.
Know it you may by many a sign;
Water is dearer far than wine;
There bread is deem'd such dainty fare,
That every prudent traveller
His wallet loads with many a crust;
For, at Canusium, you might just
As well attempt to gnaw a stone
As think to get one morsel down.
That too with scanty streams is fed:
Its founder was brave Diomed.
Good Varius (ah, that friends must part!)
Here left us all with aching heart.

At Rubi we arriv'd that day,
Well jaded by the length of way,
And sure poor mortals ne'er were wetter.
Next day, no weather could be better,
No roads so bad; we scarce could crawl
Along to fishy Barium's wall.

Th' Egnatians next, who by the rules
Of common-sense are knaves or fools,
Made all our sides with laughter heave,
Since we with them must needs believe
That incense in their temples burns
And without fire to ashes turns.
To circumcision's bigots tell
Such tales! for me, I know full well,
That in high heaven, unmov'd by care,
The Gods eternal quiet share:

Nor can I deem their spleen the cause
Why fickle Nature breaks her laws.
 Brundusium last we reach: and there
Stop short the Muse and Traveller.

William Cowper

To Bullatius

On Foreign Travel

Epistles I, 11

Do the famed islands of th' Ionian seas,
 Chios, or Lesbos, my Bullatius please?
Or Sardis, where great Croesus held his court?
Say, are they less, or greater than report?
Does Samos, Colophon, or Smyrna, yield
To our own Tiber, or to Mars's field?
Would you, fatigued with trials of lands and seas,
In Lebedus, or Asia, spend your days?
 You tell me Lebedus is now become
A desert, like our villages at home,
Yet there you gladly fix your future lot,
Your friends forgetting, by your friends forgot;
Enjoy the calm of life, and safe on shore,
At distance hear the raging tempest roar.
 A traveller, though wet with dirt and rain,
Would not forever at an inn remain,
Or chill'd with cold, and joying in the heat
Of a warm bath, believe his bliss complete.
 Though by strong winds your bark were tempest toss'd,
Say, would you sell it on a distant coast?
 Believe me, at delicious Rhodes to live,
To a sound mind no greater bliss can give,

Than a thick coat in summer's burning ray,
Or a light mantle on a snowy day,
Or to a swimmer Tiber's freezing stream,
Or sunny rooms in August's mid-day flame.
While yet 'tis in your power; while Fortune smiles,
At Rome with rapture vaunt those happy isles,
Then with a grateful hand the bliss receive,
If heaven an hour more fortunate shall give.
Seize on the present joy, and thus possess,
Where'er you live, an inward happiness.

    If reason only can our cares allay,
Not the bold site, that wide commands the sea;
If they, who through the venturous ocean range,
Not their own passions, but the climate change;
Anxious through seas and land to search for rest
Is but laborious idleness at best.
In desert Ulubrae the bliss you'll find,
If you preserve a firm and equal mind.

Philip Francis

The Country Mouse

Satires II, 6

I've often wish'd that I had clear
  For life, six hundred pounds a year,
A handsome House to lodge a Friend,
A River at my garden's end,
A terras-walk, and half a Rood
Of Land, set out to plant a Wood.
    Well, now I have all this and more,
I ask not to increase my store;
But here a Grievance seems to lie,
All this is mine but till I die;

I can't but think 'twould sound more clever,
To me and to my Heirs for ever.
  If I ne'er got, or lost a groat,
By any *Trick,* or any *Fault;*
And if I pray by Reason's rules,
And not like forty other Fools:
As thus, "Vouchsafe, oh gracious Maker!
To grant me this and t'other Acre:
Or if it be thy Will and Pleasure
Direct my Plow to find a Treasure:"
But only what my Station fits,
And to be kept in my right wits.
Preserve, Almighty Providence!
Just what you gave me, Competence:
And let me in these Shades compose
Something in Verse as true as Prose;
Remov'd from all th' ambitious Scene,
Nor puff'd by Pride, nor sunk by Spleen.
  In short, I'm perfectly content,
Let me but live on this side *Trent:*
Nor cross the Channel twice a year,
To spend six months with Statesmen here.
  I must by all means come to town,
'Tis for the Service of the Crown,
"Lewis, the Dean will be of use,
Send for him up, take no excuse."
The toil, the danger of the Seas;
Great Ministers ne'er think of these;
Or let it cost five hundred pound,
No matter where the money's found;
It is but so much more in debt,
And that they ne'er consider'd yet.
"Good Mr. Dean, go change your gown,
Let my Lord know you've come to town."
I hurry me in haste away,
Not thinking it is Levee-day;
And find his Honour in a Pound,
Hemm'd by a triple Circle round,

Chequer'd with Ribbons blue and green;
How should I thrust myself between?
Some Wag observes me thus perplext,
And smiling, whispers to the next,
"I thought the Dean had been too proud,
To justle here among a croud."
Another in a surly fit,
Tells me I have more Zeal than Wit,
"So eager to express your love,
You ne'er consider whom you shove,
But rudely press before a Duke."
I own, I'm pleas'd with this rebuke,
And take it kindly meant to show
What I desire the World should know.

I get a whisper, and withdraw;
When twenty Fools I never saw
Come with Petitions fairly penn'd,
Desiring I would stand their friend.
This, humbly offers me his Case—
That, begs my int'rest for a Place—
A hundred other Men's affairs
Like Bees are humming in my ears.
"Tomorrow my Appeal comes on,
Without your help the Cause is gone."
"The Duke expects my Lord and you,
About some great Affair, at Two."
"Put my Lord Bolingbroke in mind,
To get my Warrant quickly sign'd:
Consider, 'tis my first request."
"Be satisfy'd, I'll do my best."
Then presently he falls to teize,
"You may for certain, if you please;
I doubt not, if his Lordship knew—
And, Mr. Dean, one word from you."

'Tis (let me see) three years and more,
(October next it will be four)
Since HARLEY bid me first attend,
And chose me for an humble friend;

Wou'd take me in his coach to chat,
And question me of this and that;
As, "What's o'clock?" And, "How's the Wind?"
"Whose Chariot's that we left behind?"
Or gravely try to read the lines
Writ underneath the Country Signs;
Or, "Have you nothing new to-day
From Pope, from Parnell, or from Gay?"
Such tattle often entertains
My Lord and me as far as Stains,
As once a week we travel down
To Windsor, and again to Town,
Where all that passes, *inter nos,*
Might be proclaim'd at Charing-Cross.
    Yet some I know with envy swell,
Because they see me us'd so well:
"How think you of our Friend the Dean?
I wonder what some people mean;
My Lord and he are grown so great,
Always together, *tête à tête,*
What, they admire him for his jokes—
See but the fortune of some Folks!"
There flies about a strange report
Of some Express arriv'd at Court,
I'm stopp'd by all the fools I meet,
And catechis'd in ev'ry street.
"You, Mr. Dean, frequent the great;
Inform us, will the Emp'ror treat?
Or do the Prints and Papers lye?"
"Faith, Sir, you know as much as I."
"Ah Doctor, how you love to jest?
'Tis now no secret."—"I protest
'Tis one to me."—"Then tell us, pray,
When are the Troops to have their pay?"
And, tho' I solemnly declare
I know no more than my Lord Mayor,
They stand amaz'd, and think me grown
The closest mortal ever known.

Thus in a sea of folly toss'd,
My choicest Hours of life are lost;
Yet always wishing to retreat,
Oh, could I see my Country Seat!
There, leaning near a gentle Brook,
Sleep, or peruse some ancient Book,
And there in sweet oblivion drown
Those Cares that haunt the Court and Town.

O charming Noons! and Nights divine!
Or when I sup, or when I dine,
My Friends above, my Folks below,
Chatting and laughing all-a-row,
The Beans and Bacon set before 'em,
The Grace-cup serv'd with all decorum:
Each willing to be pleas'd, and please,
And even the very Dogs at ease!
Here no man prates of idle things,
How this or that Italian sings,
A Neighbour's Madness, or his Spouse's,
Or what's in either of the *Houses:*
But something much more our concern,
And quite a scandal not to learn:
Which is the happier, or the wiser,
A man of Merit, or a Miser?
Whether we ought to chuse our Friends,
For their own Worth, or our own Ends?
What good, or better, we may call,
And what, the very best of all?

Our Friend Dan *Prior* told, (you know)
A Tale extreamly *à propos:*
Name a Town Life, and in a trice,
He had a Story of *two Mice.*

Once on a time (so runs the Fable)
A Country Mouse, right hospitable,
Receiv'd a Town Mouse at his Board,
Just as a Farmer might a Lord.
A frugal Mouse upon the whole,
Yet lov'd his Friend, and had a Soul;

Knew what was handsome, and wou'd do't,
On just occasion, *coute qui coute*.
He brought him Bacon (nothing lean)
Pudding, that might have pleas'd a Dean;
Cheese, such as men in Suffolk make,
But wish'd it Stilton, for his sake;
Yet to his Guest tho' no way sparing,
He eat himself the Rind and paring.
Our Courtier scarce could touch a bit,
But show'd his Breeding, and his Wit,
He did his best to seem to eat,
And cry'd, "I vow you're mighty neat.
But Lord, my Friend, this savage Scene!
For God's sake, come, and live with Men:
Consider, Mice, like Men, must die,
Both small and great, both you and I:
Then spend your life in Joy and Sport,
(This doctrine, Friend, I learnt at Court.)"

   The veriest Hermit in the Nation
May yield, God knows, to strong Temptation.
Away they come, thro' thick and thin,
To a tall house near Lincoln's-Inn:
('Twas on the night of a Debate,
When all their Lordships had sate late.)

   Behold the place, where if a Poet
Shin'd in Description, he might show it,
Tell how the Moon-beam trembling falls
And tips with silver all the walls:
Palladian walls, Venetian doors,
Grotesco roofs, and Stucco floors:
But let it (in a word) be said,
The Moon was up, and Men a-bed,
The Napkins white, the Carpet red:
The Guests withdrawn had left the Treat,
And down the Mice sate, *tête à tête*.

   Our Courtier walks from dish to dish,
Tastes for his Friend of Fowl and Fish;

Tells all their names, lays down the law,
"Que ça est bon! Ah goutez ça!
That Jelly's rich, this Malmsey healing,
Pray dip your Whiskers and your Tail in."
Was ever such a happy Swain?
He stuffs and swills, and stuffs again.
"I'm quite asham'd—'tis mighty rude
To eat so much—but all's so good.
I have a thousand thanks to give—
My Lord alone knows how to live."

No sooner said, but from the Hall
Rush Chaplain, Butler, Dogs and all:
"A Rat, a Rat! clap to the door."
The Cat comes bouncing on the floor.
O for the Heart of Homer's Mice,
Or Gods to save them in a trice!
(It was by Providence, they think,
For your damn'd Stucco has no chink)
"An't please your Honour," quoth the Peasant,
"This same Dessert is not so pleasant:
Give me again my hollow Tree!
A Crust of Bread, and Liberty."

Alexander Pope

To His Farm Bailiff

Country versus Town

Epistles I, 14

G ood bailiff of my farm, that snug domain
Which makes its master feel himself again,
Which, though you sniff at it, could once support
Five hearths, and send five statesmen to the court,

Let's have a match in husbandry; we'll try
Which can do weeding better, you or I,
And see if Horace more repays the hand
That clears him of his thistles, or his land.
Though here I'm kept administering relief
To my poor Lamia's broken-hearted grief
For his lost brother, ne'ertheless my thought
Flies to my woods, and counts the distance nought.
You praise the townsman's, I the rustic's state:
Admiring others' lots, our own we hate:
Each blames the place he lives in: but the mind
Is most in fault, which ne'er leaves self behind.
A town-house drudge, for farms you used to sigh;
Now towns and shows and baths are all your cry:
But I'm consistent with myself: you know
I grumble, when to Rome I'm forced to go.
Truth is, our standards differ: what your taste
Condemns, forsooth, as so much savage waste,
The man who thinks with Horace thinks divine,
And hates the things which you believe so fine.
I know your secret: 'tis the cook-shop breeds
That lively sense of what the country needs:
You grieve because this little nook of mine
Would bear Arabian spice as soon as wine;
Because no tavern happens to be nigh
Where you can go and tipple on the sly,
No saucy flute-girl, at whose jigging sound
You bring your feet down lumbering to the ground.
And yet, methinks, you've plenty on your hands
In breaking up these long unharrowed lands;
The ox, unyoked and resting from the plough,
Wants fodder, stripped from elm and poplar bough;
You've work too at the river, when there's rain,
As, but for a strong bank, 'twould flood the plain.
Now have a little patience, you shall see
What makes the gulf between yourself and me:
I, who once wore gay clothes and well-dressed hair,
I, who, though poor, could please a greedy fair,

I, who could sit from mid-day o'er Falern,
Now like short meals and slumbers by the burn:
No shame I deem it to have had my sport;
The shame had been in frolics not cut short.
There at my farm I fear no evil eye;
No pickthank blights my crops as he goes by;
My honest neighbours laugh to see me wield
A heavy rake, or dibble my own field.
Were wishes wings, you'd join my slaves in town,
And share the rations that they swallow down:
While that sharp footboy envies you the use
Of what my garden, flocks, and woods produce.
The horse would plough, the ox would draw the car.
No; do the work you know, and tarry where you are.

John Conington

The Unwelcome Companion

Satires I, 9

Along the Sacred Street I chanced to stray
Musing I know not what, as is my way,
And wholly wrapt in thought—when up there came
A fellow scarcely known to me by name:
Grasping my hand, "My dear friend, how d'ye do?
And pray," he cried, "how wags the world with you?"
"I thank you, passing well, as times go now;
Your servant."—And with that I made my bow.
But finding him still dangle at my sleeve
Without the slightest sign of taking leave,
I turn with cold civility and say—
"Anything further, Sir, with me to-day?"
—"Nay, truce with this reserve! it is but fit
We two were friends, since I'm a brother-wit."

Here some dull compliment I stammered out,
As, "That, Sir, recommends you much no doubt."
　Vexed to the soul and dying to be gone,
I slacken now my pace, now hurry on;
And sometimes halt at once in full career,
Whispering some trifle in my lackey's ear.
But when he still stuck by me as before,—
Sweating with inward spleen at every pore,
Oh! how I longed to let my passion pass,
And sighed, Bolanus, for thy front of brass!
　Meanwhile he keeps up one incessant chat
About the streets, the houses, and all that:
Marking at last my silence—"Well," said he,
" 'Tis pretty plain you're anxious to get free:
But patience, darling Sir! so lately met—
Odslife! I cannot think of parting yet.
Inform me, whither are your footsteps bound?"
"To see (but pray don't let me drag you round)
)A friend of mine, who lies extremely ill
A mile beyond the bridge, or further still."—
"Nay then, come on! I've nothing else to do;
And as to distance, what is that—with you!"
　On hearing this, quite driven to despair,
Guess what my looks and what my feelings were!
Never did ass upon the public road,
When on his back he felt a double load,
Hang both his ears so dismal and so blank.
"In me, Sir," he continues, "to be frank,
You know not what a friend you have in store:
Viscus and Varius will not charm you more.
For as to dancing, who with me can vie?
Or who can scribble verse so fast as I?
Again, in powers of voice so much I shine
Hermogenes himself might envy mine."
　Here for a moment, puffed with self-applause,
He stopped; I took advantage of the pause:
"These toils will shorten, sure, your precious life;
Have you no loving mother, friend, or wife,

Who takes an interest in your fate?"—"Oh, no;
Thank heaven! they're all disposed of long ago."
"Good luck (thought I), by thee no longer vexed!"
So I, it seems, must be *disposed of* next:
Well, let me but at once resign my breath;
To die by inches thus were worse than death.
Now, now I see the doom approaching near,
Which once was told me by a gossip seer:
While yet a boy, the wrinkled beldam shook
Her urn, and, eyeing me with piteous look,
"Poor lad!" she cried, "no mischief shalt thou feel
Or from the poisoned bowl or hostile steel;
Nor pricking pleurisy, nor hectic cough,
Nor slow-consuming gout shall take thee off:
'Tis thy sad lot, when grown to man's estate,
To fall the victim of a puppy's prate:
Go, treasure in thy mind the truths I've sung,
And shun, if thou art wise, a chattering tongue."
    At Vesta's temple we arrived at last;
And now one quarter of the day was past—
When by the greatest luck he had, I found,
To stand a suit, and by the law was bound
Either to answer to the charges brought,
Or else to suffer judgment by default.
"I'm sorry to detain you here," he cried;
"But might I ask you just to step aside?"
"You must excuse me; legs so cramped with gout
As mine, I fear, could never stand it out:
Then, may I perish if I've skill or taste
For law; besides, you know I am in haste."—
"Faith, now you make me doubtful what to do;
Whether to sacrifice my cause or you."
"Me, by all means, Sir!—me, I beg and pray."
"Not for the world," cried me, and led the way.
Convinced all further struggle was but vain,
I follow like a captive in his train.
    "Well"—he begins afresh—"how stand you, Sir,
In the good graces of our Minister?"—

"His favourites are but few, and those select:
Never was one more nice and circumspect."
"Enough—In all such cases I'm the man
To work my way! In short, to crown your plan,
You need some second, master of his art,
To act, d'ye see, a sort of under-part.
Now what is easier?—Do but recommend
Your humble servant to this noble friend;—
And, take my word, the coast we soon should clear,
And you erelong monopolize his ear."—
"Tush! matters go not there as you suppose;
No roof is purer from intrigues like those:
Think not, if such and such surpass myself
In wealth or wit, I'm laid upon the shelf:
Each has his place assigned."—"Why, this is new
And passing strange!"—"Yet not more strange than true."—
"Gods! how you whet my wishes! well, I vow,
I long to know him more than ever now."—
—"Assail him then; the will is all you need;
With prowess such as yours, you must succeed:
He's not impregnable; but (what is worst)
He knows it, and is therefore shy at first."
"If that's his humour, trust me, I shall spare
No kind of pains to win admittance there:
I'll bribe his porter; if denied to-day,
I'll not desist, but try some other way:
I'll watch occasions—linger in his suite,
Waylay, salute, huzzah him through the street.
Nothing of consequence beneath the sun
Without great labour ever yet was done."
    Thus he proceeded prattling without end,
When—who should meet us but my worthy friend,
Aristius Fuscus, one who knew the fop
And all his humours: up he comes—we stop.
"Whence now, good Sir, and whither bound?" he cries,
And to like questions, put in turn, replies.
In hopes he'd take the hint and draw me off,
I twitch his listless sleeve—nod—wink—and cough.

He, feigning ignorance what my signals mean,
With cruel waggery smiles:—I burn with spleen.
  "Fuscus (said I), you mentioned t'other day
Something particular you wished to say
Betwixt ourselves."—"Perhaps I might: 'tis true:
But never mind; some other time will do:
This is the Jews' grand feast; and I suspect
You'd hardly like to spurn that holy sect."—
"Nay, for such scruples, 'troth I feel not any."—
"Well, but I do, and, like the vulgar many,
Am rather tender in such points as these:
So by and bye of that, Sir, if you please."—
Ah me! that e'er so dark a sun should rise!
Away the pitiless barbarian flies,
And leaves me baffled, half bereft of life,
All at the mercy of the ruthless knife.
  With hue and cry the plaintiff comes at last;
"Soho there, sirrah! whither now so fast?
Sir,"—he addressed me—"you'll bear witness here?"
"Aye, that I will," quoth I, and turned my ear.
Anon he's dragged to court; on either side
Loud shouts ensue, and uproar lords it wide:
While I, amid the hurly-burly riot,
Thanks to Apollo's care! walk off in quiet.

Francis Howes

To Maecenas

On Imitators and Critics

Epistles I, 19

If, O Maecenas, versed in lore antique,
    We may Cratinus trust, that thirsty Greek,
Never did yet a water-drinker's song
The general favour win, or keep it long.

For since the day that Bacchus of the pards
With fauns and satyrs classed us crackbrained bards,
It has been rumoured, that the Dulcet Nine
Have mostly in the morning smelt of wine.
So high does Homer wine's delights extol,
Folks will maintain he loved a brimming bowl;
And father Ennius ne'er caught up his lyre
To sing of fights, till wine had lent him fire:
"Ye that drink not, to court or change repair,
But from sweet song I charge you to forbear!"
I spoke; and bards have ever since, men say,
Toped wine all night, and reeked of it all day.

    What! if a man shall mimic Cato's air,
By naked feet, grim looks, and cloak threadbare,
Does he by this embody to our view
Cato's great character and virtues too?
Poor Codrus, bent on passing for a wit,
To give Timagenes back hit for hit,
With so much energy and passion spoke,
That in the effort a blood-vessel broke.
What mere delusion is it which reflects
A man of note by copying his defects?
Yet some would, if perchance my colour fail,
Drink cummin-wine to make themselves look pale.
O servile crew! How oft your antics mean
Have moved my laughter, oh, how oft my spleen!

    I was the first new regions to explore,
And boldly tread where none had trod before.
Who trusts himself, and leaves the beaten track,
Will soon have hosts of followers at his back.
'Twas in my measures Italy first heard
The tones Iambic of the Parian bard.
These and his spirit were my model,—not
The words that drove Lycambes all distraught;
Yet should you deck me not with scantier bays,
Because my style was modelled on his lays.
With her strong numbers Sappho blends a tone
Caught from Archilochus, to swell her own;

So too Alcaeus, though unlike, we know,
Both in his themes and in his rhythmic flow,
He neither seek a sire-in-law, on whose
Vexed head to pour the rancours of his muse,
Nor yet in fierce calumnious distichs chide,
To weave a halter for a faithless bride.
Him, too, till then by Latium's bards unsung,
I made familiar on our Roman tongue;
And 'tis my pride, that gentle hands and eyes
The strains that else had been unheard of prize.

Ask you, what makes ungracious readers laud
My works at home, and rail at them abroad?
'Tis that I will not stoop to buy men's votes
By costly dinners, or by cast-off coats;
'Tis that when men of rank their poems read,
I keep away, nor will their merits plead;
'Tis that I hold of no account the cliques
Of fussy pedants, and their sage critiques.
Hence all these tears! Were I to say, "Indeed,
For very shame I could not dare to read
Before a crowded theatre the small
And flimsy trifles from my pen that fall;"
"Oh, sir," they'd cry, "we understand the sneer;
Your works are kept for Jove's imperial ear!
You've such high notions of yourself; from you
Alone distils the pure poetic dew!"

Retort were dangerous; and my courage quails
At what might happen from my critic's nails.
So, "The ground does not suit me!" I exclaim,
And crave for a cessation of the game.
For sport like this has oft engendered rude
Intemperate wrangling, and an angry mood,—
That angry mood engendered rooted hate,
War to the knife, and an untimely fate.

Sir Theodore Martin

The Critic

Scattered through Horace's informal conversations in verse are many passages in which he discusses literary problems. Three of the Satires (I, 4 and 10; II, 1) are devoted to the poet's defense of himself from the charge of scandal-mongering and to a consideration of the nature of Roman satire. An Epistle (II, 1) addressed by imperial command to Augustus makes a comparison of ancient and modern poets and presents in brief résumé a history of dramatic verse. But the most famous of Horace's critical works is the epistle addressed to the Piso family, a father and two sons, and called, though probably not by the poet himself, The Art of Poetry. This is also the longest poem that Horace wrote.

The identity of the Pisos is not known, but from the poem itself we may infer that one of the sons was about to attempt a dramatic composition, possibly choosing a Homeric subject and modeling his work on the Greek satyr-plays.

The Art of Poetry is not what its title would seem to imply, a complete and systematic treatise, but rather a casual and discursive talk on poetry in general and dramatic poetry in particular. Its central idea is that all the arts demand a disciplined sense of propriety. A poem must have unity. Meter and diction must suit the theme or the character speaking. In dramatic poetry many elements must be brought into harmony, as may best be done by imitating Greek models. The poet must be a man of good sense, knowing human nature and devoted to high ideals, aware of the lofty nature of poetry, but not too proud to profit by impartial criticism.

Through the ages The Art of Poetry has enjoyed an enormous reputation, which, however, no longer seems justified by its intrinsic qualities. It consists of nothing more than a collection of commonplaces, many of them ultimately traceable to Aristotle. Here more than anywhere else Horace's contribution was limited to the felicitous statement of

What oft was thought, but ne'er so well expressed.

243

We recall the mountain in labor that brings forth the ridiculous mouse, the praiser of the good old times, the whetstone of genius, the nodding of Homer, all Horatian phrases that have passed into the fiber of our language.

Queen Elizabeth attempted a translation of The Art of Poetry, but made heavy weather of it and broke off after composing over two hundred halting lines. The entire poem was vigorously paraphrased by Ben Jonson. It seems appropriate, however, to reproduce here the smooth though rather flat version in blank verse by the Earl of Roscommon, since that is most nearly associated with the period in English literature when the authority of Horace was at its height. A comparison of Roscommon's translation with Pope's Essay on Criticism will show how indispensable for poems of this type was the epigrammatic rhyming couplet. It is Pope, moreover, who best sums up the quality of Horace as a literary critic:

> *Horace still charms with graceful negligence,*
> *And without method talks us into sense;*
> *Will, like a friend, familiarly convey*
> *The truest notions in the easiest way.*

To the Pisos

On the Art of Poetry

If in a picture (Piso) you should see
  A handsome woman with a fish's tail,
Or a man's head upon a horse's neck,
Or limbs of beasts of the most different kinds,
Cover'd with feathers of all sorts of birds,
Would you not laugh, and think the painter mad!
Trust me, that book is as ridiculous,
Whose incoherent style (like sick men's dreams)
Varies all shapes and mixes all extremes.
Painters and poets have been still allow'd
Their pencils, and their fancies unconfin'd.
This privilege we freely give and take;
But Nature, and the common laws of sense,
Forbid to reconcile antipathies,
Or make a snake engender with a dove,
And hungry tigers court the tender lambs.

  Some, that at first have promis'd mighty things,
Applaud themselves, when a few florid lines
Shine through th' insipid dulness of the rest;
Here they describe a temple, or a wood,
Or streams that through delightful meadows run,
And there the rainbow, or the rapid Rhine;
But they misplace them all, and crowd them in,
And are as much to seek in other things,
As he, that only can design a tree,
Would be to draw a shipwreck or a storm.
When you begin with so much pomp and show,
Why is the end so little and so low?
Be what you will, so you be still the same.
  Most poets fall into the grossest faults,
Deluded by a seeming excellence:

By striving to be short, they grow obscure,
And when they would write smoothly, they want strength,
Their spirits sink; while others, that affect
A lofty style, swell to a tympany.
Some timorous wretches start at every blast,
And, fearing tempests, dare not leave the shore;
Others, in love with wild variety,
Draw boars in waves, and dolphins in a wood:
Thus fear of erring, join'd with want of skill,
Is a most certain way of erring still.

The meanest workman in th' Aemilian square,
May grave the nails, or imitate the hair,
But cannot finish what he hath begun:
What can be more ridiculous than he?
For one or two good features in a face,
Where all the rest are scandalously ill,
Make it but more remarkably deform'd.

Let poets match their subject to their strength,
And often try what weight they can support,
And what their shoulders are too weak to bear.
After a serious and judicious choice,
Method and eloquence will never fail.

As well the force as ornament of verse
Consists in choosing a fit time for things,
And knowing when a Muse may be indulg'd
In her full flight, and when she should be curb'd.

Words must be chosen, and be plac'd with skill:
You gain your point, when by the noble art
Of good connection, an unusual word
Is made at first familiar to our ear.
But if you write of things abstruse or new,
Some of your own inventing may be us'd,
So it be seldom and discreetly done:
But he, that hopes to have new words allow'd,
Must so derive them from the Grecian spring,
As they may seem to flow without constraint.
Can an impartial reader discommend
In Varius, or in Virgil, what he likes

In Plautus or Caecilius? Why should I
Be envy'd for the little I invent,
When Ennius and Cato's copious style
Have so enrich'd, and so adorn'd our tongue?
Men ever had, and ever will have, leave
To coin new words well suited to the age.
Words are like leaves, some wither every year,
And every year a younger race succeeds.
Death is a tribute all things owe to Fate;
The Lucrine mole (Caesar's stupendous work)
Protects our navies from the raging north;
And (since Cethegus drain'd the Pontine lake)
We plough and reap where former ages row'd.
See how the Tiber (whose licentious waves
So often overflow'd the neighbouring fields)
Now runs a smooth and inoffensive course,
Confin'd by our great emperor's command:
Yet this, and they, and all, will be forgot.
Why then should words challenge eternity,
When greatest men and greatest actions die?
Use may revive the obsoletest words,
And banish those that now are most in vogue;
Use is the judge, the law, and rule of speech.

   Homer first taught the world in epic verse
To write of great commanders and of kings.

   Elegies were at first design'd for grief,
Though now we use them to express our joy:
But to whose Muse we owe that sort of verse,
Is undecided by the men of skill.

   Rage with iambics arm'd Archilochus,
Numbers for dialogue and action fit,
And favourites of the dramatic Muse;
Fierce, lofty, rapid, whose commanding sound
Awes the tumultuous noises of the pit,
And whose peculiar province is the stage.

   Gods, heroes, conquerors, Olympic crowns,
Love's pleasing cares, and the free joys of wine,
Are proper subjects for the lyric song.

Why is he honour'd with a poet's name,
Who neither knows nor would observe a rule:
And chooses to be ignorant and proud,
Rather than own his ignorance, and learn?
Let every thing have its due place and time.
    A comic subject loves an humble verse,
Thyestes scorns a low and comic style.
Yet Comedy sometimes may raise her voice,
And Chremes be allow'd to foam and rail:
Tragedians too lay by their state to grieve;
Peleus and Telephus, exil'd and poor,
Forget their swelling and gigantic words.
He that would have spectators share his grief,
Must write not only well, but movingly,
And raise men's passions to what weight he will.
We weep and laugh, as we see others do:
He only makes me sad who shows the way,
And first is sad himself; then, Telephus,
I feel the weight of your calamities,
And fancy all your miseries my own:
But, if you act them ill, I sleep or laugh;
Your looks must alter, as your subject does,
From kind to fierce, from wanton to severe:
For Nature forms, and softens us within,
And writes our fortune's changes in our face.
Pleasure enchants, impetuous rage transports,
And grief dejects, and wrings the tortur'd soul,
And these are all interpreted by speech;
But he whose words and fortunes disagree,
Absurd, unpity'd, grows a public jest.
Observe the characters of those that speak,
Whether an honest servant, or a cheat,
Or one whose blood boils in his youthful veins,
Or a grave matron, or a busy nurse,
Extorting merchants, careful husbandmen,
Argives or Thebans, Asians or Greeks.
    Follow report, or feign coherent things;
Describe Achilles, as Achilles was,

Impatient, rash, inexorable, proud,
Scorning all judges, and all law but arms;
Medea must be all revenge and blood,
Ino all tears, Ixion all deceit,
Io must wander, and Orestes mourn.

   If your bold Muse dare tread unbeaten paths,
And bring new characters upon the stage,
Be sure you keep them up to their first height.
New subjects are not easily explain'd,
And you had better choose a well-known theme
Than trust to an invention of your own:
For what originally others writ,
May be so well disguis'd, and so improv'd,
That with some justice it may pass for yours;
But then you must not copy trivial things,
Nor word for word too faithfully translate,
Nor (as some servile imitators do)
Prescribe at first such strict uneasy rules,
As you must ever slavishly observe,
Or all the laws of decency renounce.

   Begin not as th' old poetaster did,
"Troy's famous war, and Priam's fate, I sing."
In what will all this ostentation end?
The labouring mountain scarce brings forth a mouse:
How far is this from the Maeonian style?
"Muse, speak the man, who, since the siege of Troy,
So many towns, such change of manners saw."
One with a flash begins, and ends in smoke,
The other out of smoke brings glorious light,
And (without raising expectation high)
Surprises us with daring miracles,
The bloody Lestrygons, Charybdis' gulf,
And frightened Greeks, who near the Etna shore.
Hear Scylla bark, and Polyphemus roar.
He doth not trouble us with Leda's eggs,
When he begins to write the Trojan war;
Nor, writing the return of Diomed,
Go back as far as Meleager's death:

Nothing is idle, each judicious line
Insensibly acquaints us with the plot;
He chooses only what he can improve,
And truth and fiction are so aptly mix'd,
That all seems uniform, and of a piece.
　Now hear what every auditor expects;
If you intend that he should stay to hear
The epilogue, and see the curtain fall,
Mind how our tempers alter in our years,
And by that rule form all your characters.
One that hath newly learned to speak and go,
Loves childish plays, is soon provok'd and pleas'd,
And changes every hour his wavering mind.
A youth, that first casts off his tutor's yoke,
Loves horses, hounds, and sports, and exercise,
Prone to all vice, impatient of reproof,
Proud, careless, fond, inconstant, and profuse.
Gain and ambition rule our riper years,
And make us slaves to interest and power.
Old men are only walking hospitals,
Where all defects and all diseases crowd
With restless pain, and more tormenting fear,
Lazy, morose, full of delays and hopes,
Oppress'd with riches which they dare not use;
Ill-natur'd censors of the present age,
And fond of all the follies of the past.
Thus all the treasure of our flowing years,
Our ebb of life for ever takes away.
Boys must not have th' ambitious care of men,
Nor men the weak anxieties of age.
　Some things are acted, others only told;
But what we hear moves less than what we see;
Spectators only have their eyes to trust,
But auditors must trust their ears and you;
Yet there are things improper for a scene,
Which men of judgment only will relate.
Medea must not draw her murdering knife,
And spill her children's blood upon the stage,

Nor Atreus there his horrid feast prepare.
Cadmus and Progne's metamorphosis,
 (She to a swallow turn'd, he to a snake)
And whatsoever contradicts my sense,
I hate to see, and never can believe.

 Five acts are the just measure of a play.
Never presume to make a god appear,
But for a business worthy of a god;
And in one scene no more than three should speak.

 A chorus should supply what action wants,
And hath a generous and manly part;
Bridles with rage, loves rigid honesty,
And strict observance of impartial laws,
Sobriety, security, and peace,
And begs the gods who guide blind Fortune's wheel,
To raise the wretched, and pull down the proud.
But nothing must be sung between the acts,
But what some way conduces to the plot.

 First the shrill sound of a small rural pipe
 (Not loud like trumpets, nor adorn'd as now)
Was entertainment for the infant stage,
And pleas'd the thin and bashful audience
Of our well-meaning, frugal ancestors.
But when our walls and limits were enlarg'd,
And men (grown wanton by prosperity)
Study'd new arts of luxury and ease,
The verse, the music, and the scene, 's improv'd;
For how should ignorance be judge of wit,
Or men of sense applaud the jest of fools?
Then came rich clothes and graceful action in,
Then instruments were taught more moving notes,
And Eloquence with all her pomp and charms
Foretold as useful and sententious truths,
As those delivered by the Delphic god.

 The first tragedians found that serious style
Too grave for their uncultivated age,
And so brought wild and naked satyrs in,
Whose motion, words, and shape, were all a farce,

(As oft as decency would give them leave)
Because the mad ungovernable rout,
Full of confusion, and the fumes of wine,
Lov'd such variety and antic tricks.
But then they did not wrong themselves so much
To make a god, a hero, or a king,
(Stript of his golden crown and purple robe)
Descend to a mechanic dialect,
Nor (to avoid such meanness) soaring high
With empty sound and airy notions fly;
For Tragedy should blush as much to stoop
To the low mimic follies of a farce,
As a grave matron would to dance with girls:
You must not think that a satiric style
Allows of scandalous and brutish words,
Or the confounding of your characters.
Begin with Truth, then give Invention scope,
And if your style be natural and smooth,
All men will try, and hope to write as well;
And (not without much pains) be undeceiv'd.
So much good method and connection may
Improve the common and the plainest things.
A satyr, that comes staring from the woods,
Must not at first speak like an orator:
But, though his language should not be refin'd,
It must not be obscene and impudent;
The better sort abhors scurrility,
And often censures what the rabble likes.
Unpolish'd verses pass with many men,
And Rome is too indulgent in that point;
But then to write at a loose rambling rate,
In hope the world will wink at all our faults,
Is such a rash ill-grounded confidence,
As men may pardon, but will never praise.
Be perfect in the Greek originals,
Read them by day, and think of them by night.
But Plautus was admir'd in former time
With too much patience: (not to call it worse)

His harsh, unequal verse was music then,
And rudeness had the privilege of wit.
    When Thespis first expos'd the tragic Muse,
Rude were the actors, and a cart the scene,
Where ghastly faces, stain'd with lees of wine,
Frighted the children, and amus'd the crowd;
This Aeschylus (with indignation) saw,
And built a stage, found out a decent dress,
Brought visards in, (a civiler disguise)
And taught men how to speak and how to act.
Next Comedy appear'd with great applause,
Till her licentious and abusive tongue
Waken'd the magistrate's coercive power,
And forc'd it to suppress her insolence.
    Our writers have attempted every way;
And they deserve our praise, whose daring Muse
Disdain'd to be beholden to the Greeks,
And found fit subjects for her verse at home.
Nor should we be less famous for our wit,
Than for the force of our victorious arms;
But that the time and care, that are requir'd
To overlook, and file, and polish well,
Fright poets from that necessary toil.
    Democritus was so in love with wit,
And some men's natural impulses to write,
That he despis'd the help of art and rules,
And thought none poets till their brains were crackt;
And this hath so intoxicated some,
That (to appear incorrigibly mad)
They cleanliness and company renounce
For lunacy beyond the cure of art,
With a long beard, and ten long dirty nails,
Pass current for Apollo's livery.
O my unhappy stars! if in the Spring
Some physic had not cur'd me of the spleen,
None would have writ with more success than I;
But I must rest contented as I am,
And only serve to whet that wit in you,

To which I willingly resign my claim.
Yet without writing I may teach to write,
Tell what the duty of a poet is;
Wherein his wealth and ornaments consist,
And how he may be form'd, and how improv'd,
What fit, what not, what excellent or ill.
    Sound judgment is the ground of writing well;
And when Philosophy directs your choice
To proper subjects rightly understood,
Words from your pen will naturally flow;
He only gives the proper characters,
Who knows the duty of all ranks of men,
And what we owe our country, parents, friends,
How judges and how senators should act,
And what becomes a general to do;
Those are the likest copies, which are drawn
By the original or human life.
Sometimes in rough and undigested plays
We meet with such a lucky character,
As, being humour'd right, and well pursued,
Succeeds much better than the shallow verse
And chiming trifles of more studious pens.
    Greece had a genius, Greece had eloquence,
For her ambition and her end was fame.
Our Roman youth is diligently taught
The deep mysterious art of growing rich,
And the first words that children learn to speak
Are of the value of the names of coin:
Can a penurious wretch, that with his milk
Hath suck'd the basest dregs of usury,
Pretend to generous and heroic thoughts?
Can rust and avarice write lasting lines?
But you, brave youth, wise Numa's worthy heir,
Remember of what weight your judgment is,
And never venture to commend a book,
That has not pass'd all judges and all tests.
    A poet should instruct, or please, or both:
Let all your precepts be succinct and clear,

That ready wits may comprehend them soon,
And faithful memories retain them long;
All superfluities are soon forgot.
Never be so conceited of your parts,
To think you may persuade us what you please,
Or venture to bring in a child alive,
That Canibals have murder'd and devour'd.
Old age explodes all but mortality;
Austerity offends aspiring youths;
But he that joins instruction with delight,
Profit with pleasure, carries all the votes:
These are the volumes that enrich the shops,
These pass with admiration through the world,
And bring their author to eternal fame.
   Be not too rigidly censorious,
A string may jar in the best master's hand,
And the most skilful archer miss his aim;
But in a poem elegantly writ,
I would not quarrel with a slight mistake,
Such as our nature's frailty may excuse;
But he that hath been often told his fault,
And still persists, is as impertinent
As a musician that will always play,
And yet is always out at the same note:
When such a positive abandon'd fop
(Among his numerous absurdities)
Stumbles upon some tolerable lines,
I fret to see them in such company,
And wonder by what magic they came there.
But in long works sleep will sometimes surprise;
Homer himself hath been observ'd to nod.
   Poems, like pictures, are of different sorts,
Some better at a distance, others near,
Some love the dark, some choose the clearest light,
And boldly challenge the most piercing eye;
Some please for once, some will for ever please.
But, Piso, (though your knowledge of the world,
Join'd with your father's precepts, make you wise)

Remember this as an important truth:
Some things admit of mediocrity,
A counsellor, or pleader at the bar,
May want Messala's powerful eloquence,
Or be less read than deep Cascellius;
Yet this indifferent lawyer is esteem'd;
But no authority of gods nor men
Allow of any mean in poesy.
As an ill concert, and a coarse perfume,
Disgrace the delicacy of a feast,
And might with more discretion have been spar'd;
So poesy, whose end is to delight,
Admits of no degrees, but must be still
Sublimely good, or despicably ill.
In other things men have some reason left,
And one that cannot dance, or fence, or run,
Despairing of success, forbears to try;
But all (without consideration) write;
Some thinking, that th' omnipotence of wealth
Can turn them into poets when they please.
But, Piso, you are of too quick a sight
Not to discern which way your talent lies,
Or vainly with your genius to contend;
Yet if it ever be your fate to write,
Let your productions pass the strictest hands,
Mine and your father's, and not see the light
Till time and care have ripen'd every line.
What you keep by you, you may change and mend,
But words once spoke can never be recall'd.
    Orpheus, inspir'd by more than human power,
Did not, as poets feign, tame savage beasts,
But men as lawless and as wild as they,
And first dissuaded them from rage and blood.
Thus, when Amphion built the Theban wall,
They feign'd the stones obey'd his magic lute:
Poets, the first instructors of mankind,
Brought all things to their proper native use;
Some they appropriated to the gods,

And some to public, some to private ends;
Promiscuous love by marriage was restrain'd,
Cities were built, and useful laws were made;
So great was the divinity of verse,
And such observance to a poet paid.
Then Homer's and Tyrtaeus' martial Muse
Waken'd the world, and sounded loud alarms.
To verse we owe the sacred oracle,
And our best precepts of morality;
Some have by verse obtain'd the love of kings,
(Who with the Muses ease their weary'd minds)
Then blush not, noble Piso, to protect
What gods inspire, and kings delight to hear.
Some think that poets may be form'd by Art,
Others maintain that Nature makes them so;
I neither see what Art without a vein,
Nor Wit without the help of Art can do,
But mutually they crave each other's aid.
He that intends to gain th' Olympic prize
Must use himself to hunger, heat, and cold,
Take leave of wine, and the soft joys of love;
And no musician dares pretend to skill,
Without a great expense of time and pains;
But every little busy scribbler now
Swells with the praises which he gives himself;
And, taking sanctuary in the crowd,
Brags of his impudence, and scorns to mend.
A wealthy poet takes more pains to hire
A flattering audience, than poor tradesmen do
To persuade customers to buy their goods.
'Tis hard to find a man of great estate,
That can distinguish flatterers from friends.
Never delude yourself, nor read your book
Before a brib'd and fawning auditor,
For he'll commend and feign an ecstasy,
Grow pale or weep, do any thing to please:
True friends appear less mov'd than counterfeit;
As men that truly grieve at funerals,

Are not so loud as those that cry for hire.
Wise were the kings who never chose a friend,
Till with full cups they had unmask'd his soul,
And seen the bottom of his deepest thoughts;
You cannot arm yourself with too much care
Against the smiles of a designing knave.
   Quintilius ('f his advice were ask'd)
Would freely tell you what you should correct,
Or, if you could not, bid you blot it out,
And with more care supply the vacancy;
But if he found you fond and obstinate,
(And apter to defend than mend your faults)
With silence leave you to admire yourself,
And without rival hug your darling book.
The prudent care of an impartial friend
Will give you notice of each idle line,
Show what sounds harsh, and what wants ornament,
Or where it is too lavishly bestow'd;
Make you explain all that he finds obscure,
And with a strict inquiry mark your faults;
Nor for these trifles fear to lose your love:
Those things which now seem frivolous and slight,
Will be of a most serious consequence,
When they have made you once ridiculous.
   A poetaster, in his raging fit,
(Follow'd and pointed at by fools and boys)
Is dreaded and proscrib'd by men of sense;
They make a lane for the polluted thing,
And fly as from th' infection of the plague,
Or from a man whom, for a just revenge,
Fanatic Phrenzy, sent by Heaven, pursues.
If (in the raving of a frantic Muse)
And minding more his verses than his way,
Any of these should drop into a well,
Though he might burst his lungs to call for help,
No creature would assist or pity him,
But seem to think he fell on purpose in.
Hear how an old Sicilian poet dy'd;

Empedocles, mad to be thought a god,
In a cold fit leap'd into Etna's flames.
Give poets leave to make themselves away;
Why should it be a greater sin to kill,
Than to keep men alive against their will?
Nor was this chance, but a deliberate choice;
For if Empedocles were now reviv'd,
He would be at his frolic once again,
And his pretentions to divinity:
'Tis hard to say whether for sacrilege,
Or incest, or some more unheard-of crime,
The rhyming fiend is sent into these men;
But they are all most visibly possest,
And, like a baited bear when he breaks loose,
Without distinction seize on all they meet;
None ever scap'd that came within their reach,
Sticking like leeches, till they burst with blood,
Without remorse insatiably they read,
And never leave till they have read men dead.

Wentworth Dillon, Earl of Roscommon

Glossary

To His Lyre

A Lesbian poet: Alcaeus, Greek lyric poet of *c.* 600 B.C.

Melpomene

Melpomene: one of the nine Muses, specifically the Muse of tragic
poetry.

The Poet's Prayer to Apollo

libation: a small quantity of wine poured on the ground as a cere-
monial offering to a god. *Liris:* a river in Italy between Latium and
Campania. *Latona:* the gods Apollo and Diana were the children
of Jupiter and Latona.

Vocation

Olympian race: the chariot race at the Olympic games. *palm:* the
token of victory. *triple powers:* the three elective offices of the
Roman state, culminating in the consulship. *Myrtoan:* from the
island of Myrto in the western Aegean sea. *arbute:* the arbutus tree.
Euterpe, Polyhymnia: Muses representative of lyric poetry.

To Maecenas

Numantian wars: Numantia was a town in Spain conquered by the
Romans in 133 B.C. after a famous resistance. *Sicilian tide:* an epi-
sode in the First Punic War, 260 B.C. *fierce Pirithoan stir:* the battle
of the Centaurs and the Lapithae, headed by their king Pirithous.
giant sieges: wars of the giants and the gods, in which Hercules
played a leading part. *our Caesar:* Augustus. *Licymnia:* supposed to
be *Terentia,* the capricious wife of Maecenas.

To a Roman Historian

Metellus: consul in 60 B.C., when the Roman civil wars began with the breaking of the First Triumvirate, the league formed by Caesar, Pompey, and Crassus. *Attic buskin:* Greek tragedy. *Cato's iron fortitude:* the younger Cato was famous for his devotion to the Roman Republic and for his suicide when the triumph of Julius Caesar became inevitable. *Jugurtha's grave:* Jugurtha was a king of Numidia, who had long held out against Roman arms. *Daunian:* Roman. *the Cean's lofty dirge:* Simonides of Ceos wrote the epitaphs on the heroes of Thermopylae and Salamis. *Dione:* Venus.

A Truce to History

Aeacus: son of Jupiter, grandfather of Achilles. *Inachus:* first mythical king of Argos.

No Pindaric Strain

Pindar's ways: Pindar is generally considered the greatest of the Greek lyric poets for his lofty style. *Daedalean fame:* Daedalus constructed waxen wings with which his son Icarus flew so high that the wax melted and he fell to his death in the Icarian sea. *Chimaera:* a fire-breathing monster, killed by Bellerophon mounted on the winged horse Pegasus. *Elean palm:* the symbol of victory in the Olympic games. *Theban swan:* Pindar. *Sygambria's victor:* Augustus, who had just avenged the defeat of M. Lollius by the Sygambri.

To a Roman Admiral

Agrippa: a brilliant commander under Augustus and winner of several naval victories, including that at Actium. *Pelides:* Achilles, son of Peleus. *Merion:* charioteer of the Greek hero Idomeneus. *Diomede:* another Greek hero in the Trojan war, who with the help of Minerva wounded Mars and Venus.

Undying Words, Undying Worth

Stesichorus: Greek poet, *c.* 600 B.C., the chief relater of heroic legends between Homer and Pindar. *Anacreon:* much Alexandrian light verse was attributed to this Greek poet. *Aeolian maiden's poesy:* Sappho's poems. *Teucer:* the best archer among the Greeks who laid siege to Troy. *Idomeneus:* leader of the Cretans in Homer. *Sthenelos:* charioteer of Diomede. *Deiphobus:* a Trojan leader, brother of Hector.

The Gift of the Muse

Parrhasius: famous Greek painter. *Scopas:* a sculptor. *Ilia:* mother of Romulus. *Muses of Calabria:* the Latin poems of Ennius. *sons of Tyndarus:* the demi-gods Castor and Pollux. *Styx:* a river in Hades. *Liber:* Bacchus, god of wine.

His Monument

Vestal: a priestess of Vesta, whose temple stood on the Roman Capitol. *Daunus:* mythical king of Apulia, where Horace was born. *Delphic bay:* the crown of laurel leaves symbolic of recognition as a poet.

The Happy Isles

the Marsian nation: leaders of the Social War of 91 B.C., when an attempt was made to destroy Rome. *Tuscan Porsena:* Lars Porsena of Clusium, who in spite of brave Horatius captured Rome. *Capua's rivalry:* the town of Capua made an alliance with Hannibal and aspired to become the chief city of Italy. *Spartacus:* leader of gladiators who plundered Italy about 73 B.C. *Gallic rebel:* Allobrox, treacherous chieftain of the Allobroges. *Quirinus:* a name for Romulus, now deified. *Phocaea:* the people of Phocaea (534 B.C.) migrated rather than submit to Harpagus, the general of Cyrus. *Argo:* the ship in which the mythical Jason voyaged in search of the golden fleece. *dame of Colchis:* Medea.

The Ship of State

Cyclades: islands of the Greek Archipelago surrounding Delos; beautiful but dangerous.

Before Actium

Actium: the naval battle which crushed the power of Cleopatra, 31 B.C.

At the Battle

son of Neptune: Sextus Pompeius, lately defeated at the battle of Naulochus, had proclaimed himself the son of the sea-god. *Syrtes:* two gulfs on the north African coast reputed dangerous to navigation. *Lyaeus:* Bacchus.

The Death of Cleopatra

Mareotic: a sweet Egyptian wine, "the juice of Aegypt's grape."

Augustus, Guardian of Rome

Proteus: a sea-god. *Pyrrha:* Deucalion and Pyrrha, in Greek mythology, were the human pair that survived the flood. *Numa's tomb:* the order of Vestals was founded by Numa Pompilius, whose tomb was near the temple of Vesta.

The Poet's Conversion

Atlas: the giant who upheld the sky on his shoulders.

To Apollo and Diana

Delian deity: Apollo.

Light-Footed and Light-Fingered Mercury

Priam: fabled king of Troy.

Bacchus the Divine

Crown: the constellation known as Ariadne's crown. *Lycurgus:* for his opposition to the Bacchic rites Lycurgus was blinded and destroyed by the gods. *Pentheus:* a king of Thebes, who was torn to pieces by his mother and sisters in their Bacchic frenzy. *Maenades:* women devotees of the god Bacchus. *Giant gang:* after the defeat of the Titans the earth-born giants waged war on the gods of Olympus. *Cerberus:* watchdog of Hades.

Bacchic Frenzy

Semele: mother of Bacchus. *Naiad:* a nymph.

Gods and Heroes

Clio: Muse of history. *Helicon,* etc.: mountains associated with Greek legend. *Orpheus:* the mythical first poet and sweet singer of Greece. *Alcides:* Hercules. *twins of Leda:* Castor and Pollux. *Paulus:* a Roman consul who sought to die on the field of Cannae (216 B.C.) after the battle had been lost by the rashness of his colleague. *Camillus:* by his capture of Veii (390 B.C.) Camillus delivered Rome from the invading Gauls. *Marcellus:* an older Marcellus took Syracuse in 212 B.C.; a younger Marcellus was the husband of Augustus' daughter Julia and died in 23 B.C. *Seres:* an oriental tribe.

The Return of Augustus

Plancus' consulship: Plancus was consul in 42 B.C. when Horace took part in the battle of Philippi; the phrase has become proverbial for the giddy time of youth.

To Apollo

Niobe: mother of seven sons and seven daughters, whose children were killed by Apollo and Diana because she had boasted herself greater than their mother Latona. *Tityos:* a giant traditionally condemned to Hades. *Ilion:* Troy. *Sea-Thetis:* a marine goddess who was the mother of Achilles. *Dardan:* Greek. *Eurus:* the east wind. *Thalia:* one of the Muses. *Daunian Muse:* Latin poetry. *Delia:* Diana. *Leto:* Latona.

The Secular Hymn

Lucina: the name by which Diana was addressed as goddess of childbirth. *Parcae:* the three Fates. *bourn:* a refuge. *Anchises:* the Trojan father of Aeneas. *Palatine, Aventine:* two of the seven hills of Rome. *Fifteen:* priests of the sacred college in charge of religious ceremonies.

An Eagle of the Claudian Race

a young eagle: Drusus, the younger step-son of Augustus, fought and defeated the Rhaetians, crossed the Brenner pass, and broke the power of the Breuni and Genauni in the valley of the Inn. *Ganymede:* a youth snatched up to heaven by the eagle of Jupiter to become cupbearer of the gods. *Vindelici:* one of the Alpine tribes. *Neros:* Drusus and his brother Tiberius were sons of the empress Livia by her divorced husband Tiberius Claudius Nero. *Metaurus:* a river in Italy. *Punic:* Carthaginian. *Ausonian:* Italian.

Drusus and Tiberius

the elder Nero: Tiberius. *appanage:* possession.

Thanksgiving for Peace

the Janus of Quirinus: the gates of the temple of Janus were closed by Augustus on three different occasions to signify that the Roman world was at peace. *Tanais:* the Don river.

The City Farmer

Priapus, Sylvanus: rustic gods. *Morecraft:* the name in the original is Alfius. *shelf:* reef, where his good intentions are shipwrecked.

A Winter Party

Soracte: a small mountain twenty-six miles north of Rome.

Northern Exposure

cleugh: a den between rocks. *ilka:* every. *scar:* a bare place on the side of a hill. *slap:* a gap between two hills. *whins:* furze bushes. *gowfer:* golfer. *dousser fowk:* more sedate people. *wysing a-jee:* inclining in a curve. *byast bouls:* lawn bowls with a bias. *green:* bowling green. *ripe the ribs:* poke the fire through the bars of the fireplace. *beek the house,* etc.: heat the house from one end to the other. *mutchkin stoup:* pint measure. *dribs:* drops. *Tappit hen:* the Scots quart measure or half-gallon. *gash:* wise. *rowth:* plenty. *fashious:* troublesome. *wood:* mad. *quate:* quiet. *blatt'ring:* rattling.

cour: creep. *neist:* next. *feckless:* feeble. *quat the grip:* let go of. *twafold o'er a rung:* doubled over. *gowan:* daisy. *a the wyte:* all the blame. *kepp ony skaith:* take any harm. *haith:* hey! *rook:* thief. *nineteen nay-says,* etc.: nineteen refusals are half a consent. *toolie:* contend. *whop:* snatch. *taiken:* token. *carlies:* old men. *whisht:* hush, be silent.

Retirement

Galaesus: a stream in southern Italy, near Tarentum.

Come Home to Tibur

pillioned: riding as on a saddle. *Pallas' city:* Athens. *Lacedaemon:* Sparta. *Albunea's echoing cavern:* the grotto of the old Italian oracle connected with the last of the Sibyls. *Teucer:* a Greek warrior from Salamis, who dared not return home from Troy after the suicide of his half-brother Ajax Telamon, but led his followers to conquer Cyprus.

An American Paraphrase

Ierne: Ireland. *Ab'rams Plains:* near Quebec, where Wolfe and Montcalm fought the decisive battle of the French and Indian War. *Kent:* a county in Delaware. *farmer:* John Dickinson, author of Letters from a Farmer in Pennsylvania, 1767, a moderate Revolutionary patriot. *West:* Benjamin West, an American painter who successfully established himself in London, and so compared to Apelles, the most famous painter of antiquity. *Muses' Seat:* the colleges of Philadelphia and Princeton (author's note), *Boston's police:* (pronounce póll-is) civil government in general. *N--- C----e:* Newcastle, Pa. *inemulous:* unambitious.

Accursed Tree

Colchos breed: associated with the baneful sorceress Medea. *Aeacus:* judge of the dead. *euer-blushing meads:* the Elysian Fields, abode of happy souls. *hundred-headed beast:* Cerberus, watchdog of Hades, usually said to be three-headed. *lugges:* ears. *curl'd snakes:* the Furies were supposed to have serpents for hair. *Pelops sterved sire:* Tantalus, tormented in Hades by the sight of food and drink that he could not get. *Orion:* the famous hunter of Greek legend.

Hymn for the Neptunalia

Nereides: sea-nymphs. *Cynthia:* Diana. *Her who Cnidos sees:* Venus.

The Anniversary

falling tree: see Accursed Tree above. *rosin seals:* wine was sealed in jars, not corked in bottles. *Dacian Cottiso:* one of the allies of Antony.

To Aristius Fuscus

mad Celestial Dog: Sirius, the dog-star, supposed to be responsible for summer heats. *wan:* won.

Bon Voyage for Virgil

Twin Stars: Castor and Pollux, sons of Jupiter; the reference is probably to the corposants or St. Elmo's fire, thought to be a lucky sign. *he who rules the raging wind:* Aeolus, god of the winds. *Prometheus:* in Greek mythology a beneficent Titan who against the command of Jupiter taught mankind the use of fire. *Alcides:* Hercules.

Comrade in Arms

Lethe: a river in Hades which caused the dead to forget their lives on earth.

In Praise of Lamia

Bear: the constellation of the Great Bear or the Dipper. *Tiridates:* a king of Parthia, whom Augustus was aiding against his rival Phraates. *Lesbian quill:* a poem modeled on the Greek lyrics of Alcaeus and Sappho.

A Feast for a Rainy Day

augury: prophecy; certain birds were supposed to foresee coming events.

To a Jar of Wine

Manlius' consulate: 65 B.C., the year of Horace's birth. *Corvinus:* M. Valerius Messala, who had been a fellow-student with Horace at Athens.

Invitation to Maecenas

delf: pottery. *her oldest flood:* the river Tiber. *Cajeta's grape:* famous vintages, such as Calenian and Formian wine.

Love's the Alibi

Teian bard: the Greek poet Anacreon.

Not to Be Parted

Chimera, Gyas, etc.: monsters of the underworld.

Maecenas' Birthday

Ides: the mid day of the month, here April 13. *daughter of the main:* Venus, who was said to have risen from the sea. *Phaethon:* son of Apollo, who tried unsuccessfully to drive the chariot of the sun. *Pegasus:* the winged horse on which the hero Bellerophon sought to ride.

To Vergilius

luckless bird: according to Greek myth, Procne, daughter of the royal house of Cecrops, served up her own son Itys as a feast for her husband, King Tereus, to avenge his cruelties to herself and his violation of her sister Philomela. The latter was transformed into a nightingale, while Procne became a swallow. *nard:* a perfumed ointment.

A Proper Feast

Charybdis: a whirlpool dangerous to mariners near the straits of Messina.

A Stormy Night for Revelry

Torquatus' consulate: 65 B.C. *Centaur:* Cheiron, the wise horseman who educated Achilles. *Thetis:* mother of Achilles. *Assaracus's realm:* the plains of Troy, watered by the Simois and the Scamander.

To Torquatus

lie: at Roman banquets the guests reclined on couches. *elude the guard:* Torquatus as a busy lawyer would be obliged to slip away from his importunate clients.

Love Mocks Us All

Hadria's tide: the stormy Adriatic.

To Pyrrha

sacred wall: Neptune's temple, where a sailor who had escaped from shipwreck might hang a votive picture or some token of his deliverance.

A Tale to Touch the Heart

tortoise-shell: the lyre, first made by stretching strings across the hollow shell of a tortoise. *vasty forecourt's guard:* Cerberus, the watchdog of Hades. *that urn:* the daughters of Danaus, who with one exception had assisted their father in the treacherous slaying of their husbands, were condemned to fill a leaky cask with water.

To Lydia

Notus: the south wind.

"Tears, Idle Tears . . ."

Oricus: the lover is winter-bound in the harbor of Oricum in Epirus, where he is impatiently waiting to cross the Adriatic.

Integer Vitae

Syrtes, Caucasus, Hydaspes: regions notoriously inhospitable to man. *Juba's sand:* Mauritania.

The Satirist's Recantation

Thyestes' race: one of the earlier atrocities connected with the house of Atreus in Greek legend was the banquet of Thyestes, whose sons were served to him as food.

Invitation to Tyndaris

the hero: Ulysses.

Lastly to Venus

sower: sour. *livor:* one who knows how to live. *fyl's his tongue:* speaks eloquently. *Ensignes:* insignia, banners.

Priapus and the Witches

Hecate, Tisiphone: goddesses of the underworld.

The Orgy

coil: elaborate preparations. *bulla:* the amulet worn by free-born boys. *flags not:* does not tire. *Creon's haughty child:* Glauce, the bride of Jason, whom the sorceress Medea destroyed by means of a poisoned garment. *Nepenthe:* a drug that alleviates pain and sorrow. *Manes:* spirits of the dead.

Poet and Witch

Nereus' grandson: Achilles, who magnanimously healed the wound of his foe. *the poet:* Stesichorus was blinded by the demi-gods Castor and Pollux for insulting their sister Helen of Troy in his verse. He wrote a recantation and his sight was restored. *Cotytto:* a Thracian sorceress. *Pelignian hags:* her teachers in witchcraft.

The Upstart

the holy way: the Via Sacra, a street in Rome. *Otho's laws:* the regulations which assigned seats in the theater according to social rank.

A Pleasant Voyage for Maevius

Ajax' impious bark: the ship was accursed because it bore the priestess Cassandra carried off by force from her temple.

Praise of Meane and Constant Estate

Thomas: Sir Thomas Wyatt, a fellow-poet. *freat:* rub. *halseth:* embraces. *aduisedly:* intentionally. *disdayn:* envy. *glome:* glower. *riues:* splits. *falne:* fall down. *stepe:* high. *cliues:* cliffs. *hart well stayd:* steadfast heart. *ouerthwartes deep:* serious misfortunes. *Now ill, not aye thus:* if things are now bad, they will not always be so. *once Phebus,* etc.: once Phoebus shall cease to frown and unstring his bow. *straite estate:* difficulties. *ryft:* reef in the sail. *hast is wast,* etc.: it will be proved that haste is waste.

"Draw In Thy Swelling Sailes"

foreworne house: ruinous house. *snarde:* snared. *doome:* judgment.

On Serenity

Descended: the Ode is addressed to Maecenas, whose famous ancestry Horace is careful to mention here as elsewhere. *Lion:* the sign of Leo in the Zodiac. *Syrian star:* Sirius, the dog-star.

Fie on Eastern Luxury!

linden twine: ready-made garlands sewn on linden bark could be bought at the shops.

Chicago Analogue

loophound: a frequenter of Chicago's Loop district.

Money Is Not to Keep

Proculeius: the brother of Maecenas' wife, who shared his property with his brothers when they forfeited their estates in the civil wars. *Phraates:* a pretender to the throne of Parthia.

No Gilded Roof Is Mine

vaine: vein. *Baiae:* a Roman summer colony near Naples, where villas were often built out over the sea.

Choose Moderate Riches

Danaë: the daughter of King Acrisius of Argos, immured in a tower because it was prophesied that her son would slay her father, was visited by Jupiter in the guise of a shower of gold and became the mother of Perseus. *Philip's march:* King Philip of Macedon is said to have remarked that any fortress could be taken if it could be reached by an ass laden with gold.

Wealth Encroaches

planes: plane trees, good only for shade. *chance-cut turf:* an altar of piled turf sufficed for worship in the good old days; now we must have ostentatious temples of marble.

To the Covetous

palace keeps: treasure vaults.

Ilium Fuit, Roma Est

Acheron's wave: a river in Hades. *judge accurst:* Prince Paris of Troy, who adjudged that the golden apples should be given to Venus, was rewarded by the love of Helen, the "stranger dame." *a grandson:* Romulus, son of Mars and the priestess Ilia.

The Voice of the Muse

Palinurus' cliff: a headland on the Sicilian coast, where the steersman of Aeneas fell overboard and was drowned. *Rhoetus, etc.:* names of the giants who assailed the gods of Olympus. *Pirithous:* bound with chains in Hades because he attempted with Theseus to carry off Prosperpina, the queen of the underworld.

The True Roman Temper

Crassus: a member of the First Triumvirate, was killed and his army defeated by the Parthians in 53 B.C. This disgrace to Roman arms was still unavenged. *Regulus:* Roman consul captured by the Carthaginians in 255 B.C. and sent to Rome to treat for peace or to arrange for an exchange of prisoners. He advised the Senate to refuse both proposals, though he knew that he was signing his death warrant by so doing. *Punic:* Carthaginian.

Honor the Gods

Labienus: one of Julius Caesar's generals in Gaul, who fought on the side of Pompey in the civil wars and was killed at the battle of Munda, 45 B.C.

Consolation to Valgius

the old man: Nestor, the sage and hero of the Greeks at Troy, was the father of Antilochus. *Troilus:* a son of King Priam and brother of Hector. *Niphates:* a mountain in Armenia. *the Mede's haughty river:* the Don.

The Ghost of Archytas to the Sailor

a little want thereof: sand must be scattered on the corpse before the spirit of the dead could proceed to its place in the underworld. *Pelops' sire:* Tantalus. *Tithonus:* lover of the goddess Aurora. *Minos:* king of Crete. *Pythagoras:* the Greek hero Euphorbus was supposed to have been reincarnated as the philosopher Pythagoras.

The Stoic

the dark urn: lots were cast by shaking them from a vase.

Vision of Death

Cocytus: a river in Hades.

Mortality

Hippolytus: a virtuous youth, slain by his stepmother Phaedra, whose advances he scorned. *Theseus:* freed from Hades by Hercules, but unable to free his comrade Pirithous.

Dust and Dreams

Tullus, etc.: examples of the wealthy, the good, and the pious.

Good Birth—and What of It?

squinnied: wrinkled up in disdain. *Tullius:* Tullius Severus, one of the legendary kings of Rome. *Laevinus:* a man of excellent family but "not worth a cent" in an election. *Syrus,* etc.: three familiar names for slaves. *Tarpeian rock:* criminals were sometimes executed by being hurled down from this cliff. *Paulus, Messala:* aristocratic names. *Satureian countryside:* the district near Tarentum. *fasces, curule chair:* symbols of office. *Marsyas' statue:* the spot in the Forum where law business was transacted. *quaestor:* the lowest of the state offices which ennobled the holders.

To Maecenas

Latian festival: the Feriae Latinae or great common festival of the early Latin communities, held on the Alban Mount.

The Journey to Brundusium

Aricia, Appii Forum, etc.: towns along the Appian Way. *Cocceius:* a Roman noble, great-grandfather of the Emperor Nerva. *Plotius:* a literary friend of Varius and Virgil. *the bard:* Virgil, who was born at Mantua. *Nine:* the nine Muses. *Lares:* the official guardian spirits of the state. *Apulian hills:* Horace was born in this region. *circumcision's bigots:* the Jews.

To Bullatius

desert Ulubrae: a dull village in the Pontine marshes, equivalent to "the sticks."

The Country Mouse

the Channel: St. George's Channel between Ireland and England.
the Dean: Pope has transposed the poem into terms of his own
time; in place of Horace he has substituted Jonathan Swift, Dean of
St. Patrick's, and for Maecenas the English statesmen, Lord Boling-
broke and Lord Oxford (Harley). *Ribbons:* the insignia of the
orders of the Bath and the Garter. *Pope, etc.:* three poets of the
Queen Anne period, friends of Swift. *proclaim'd at Charing Cross:*
announced publicly in London. *Express:* courier. *Houses:* Houses
of Parliament. *Prior:* Matthew Prior, author of graceful society
verse. *Stilton:* the best English cheese. *Malmsey:* a kind of wine.
Homer's Mice: an allusion to the mock-epic Battle of the Frogs
and Mice, attributed to Homer.

To His Farm Bailiff

five statesmen: the five families of Horace's tenants were entitled to
send five representatives to the local court. *husbandry:* farming.
here: in Rome. *burn:* brook.

The Unwelcome Companion

Bolanus: a quick-tempered man who would have disposed of the
bore in no time. *Viscus and Varius:* literary men and close friends of
Horace. *Hermogenes:* Horace's ideal of effeminacy and bad
taste. *turned my ear:* a person summoned as a witness allowed the
tip of his ear to be touched as a sign of his willingness to testify.

To Maecenas

Cratinus: a writer of Greek comedies in the time of Pericles and a
notorious drunkard. *of the pards:* the god Bacchus was traditionally
drawn in his chariot by a team of leopards. *Dulcet Nine:* the Muses.
Cato's air: Cato the Censor was famous for his grim morality.
Parian bard: Archilochus, whom Horace imitated in his Epodes.

To the Pisos

tympany: inflated language, bombast. *Plautus:* Roman playwright
and writer of comedies. *Caecilius:* chief comic dramatist in succes-

sion to Plautus. *Ennius:* one of the greatest of early Roman poets, who died about a hundred years before Horace was born. *Chremes:* the angry father of the comic stage. *Peleus and Telephus:* tragic heroes in distress. *Ino:* in Greek mythology, daughter of Cadmus and Harmonia, transformed into a sea-goddess. *Ixion:* a Thessalian who for his atrocious crimes was fastened to a perpetually turning wheel in Hades. *Orestes:* son of Agamemnon and Clytemnestra, who avenged his father's murder by killing his mother. *Maeonian:* Homeric. *Lestrygons, Polyphemus,* etc.: episodes in the adventures of Ulysses. *Leda's eggs:* Jupiter wooed Leda in the form of a swan; hence she laid the eggs from which sprang Castor and Pollux. *Meleager's death:* his life depended on a magic brand; when he angered his mother, she put the brand on the fire and as soon as it was consumed Meleager died. *Cadmus:* founder of Thebes and legendary inventor of the alphabet; he and his wife Harmonia were changed into serpents. *Democritus:* Greek philosopher. *Messala:* member of an aristocratic family and a former supporter of the Roman Republic; a distinguished orator, author, and patron of letters. *Amphion:* legendary builder of the walls of Thebes, drawing the stones into place by the compulsion of his harping. *Tyrtaeus:* a poet of Sparta (7th century B.C.). *Quintilius:* Quintilius Varus, a critic friend of Catullus and Virgil. *Empedocles:* a Sicilian philosopher and scientist, who according to tradition leaped into the fiery crater of Etna.

List of Poems

in the traditional order

Index of Translators